Cracking the Corporate Culture Code

Unwritten Ground Rules

Steve Simpson

Published by Narnia House Publishing
PO Box 554
Sanctuary Cove 4212
Queensland, Australia

Phone: +61 (0)7 5530 1465
Fax: +61 (0)7 5530 1295
E-mail: info@keystone-management.com

This edition printed 2007
Second edition printed 2005
First published 2001
Copyright © 2001 Steve Simpson

This book is copyright. Apart from any fair dealing for the purpose of private study, research, criticism or review, as permitted under the Copyright Act, no part may be reproduced by any process without written permission from the publisher.

All effort was made to render this book free from error and omission. However, the author, publisher, editor, their employees or agents shall not accept responsibility for injury, loss or damage to any person or body or organisation acting or refraining from action as a result of material in this book, whether or not such injury, loss or damage is in any way due to any negligent act or omission, breach of duty, or default on the part of the author, publisher, editor or their employees or agents.

UGRs® is a registered trademark and cannot be used without express permission from Keystone Management Services.

National Library Cataloguing In Publication Data:

Simpson, Stephen
UGRs: Cracking the Corporate Culture Code

ISBN 0-9579316-0-3

1. Corporate culture. 2. Customer services. 3. Organizational effectiveness. I. Title.

This book is dedicated to my father:

Albie Simpson

A man who was much loved and who inspired many.

Acknowledgments

I would like to recognise and thank the people who gave me professional support in writing and compiling this book:

- Wendy Eriksson – for her layout and design expertise, applied during an ever-decreasing timeline!
- Bert Pierce – for his wonderful illustrations
- Rachel Rogers – for her great ability to pick up on my typing, grammar and other errors

Foreword

Organizational culture and customer service are two of the most important areas that every organization needs to get right for them to survive and prosper. This book provides you with a clear way to understand the complex phenomenon of culture and helps you take some important and vital steps to change your culture in a way that contributes to your key business objectives.

Over the last 20 years I have worked as a management consultant with a large number of public and private sector organizations including mining companies, banks, property developers and not-for-profit companies. The major areas I have focused on are leadership and organisational change. I am certain that Steve Simpson has discovered a simple yet profound approach to organizational culture that can be of tremendous value to managers and human resource professionals who genuinely want to shift their team to a more positive culture that is beneficial to their customers and the staff with whom they work.

Cont...

I was very pleased to be asked by Steve to write a foreword to 'UGRs: Cracking the Corporate Culture Code'. This book, and Steve's extraordinary commitment to customer service are a valuable contribution to our understanding and transforming of organizational culture.

Dr Ron Cacioppe

Managing Director
Senior Management Centre
AIM and UWA

Professor
Graduate School of Management
University of Western Australia

September 2001

Imagine that........

You have never been in a motor vehicle. The first time you are shown one, you are overwhelmed. You are truly impressed to get into a transport vehicle that has so many features – air conditioning, heating, CD player, electric windows, sun roof, automatic transmission.

With a little help, you work out how to start the car. Unbeknown to you it is running on three, rather than four cylinders. Having never driven a car before, you don't know the difference. You think this is 'normal'. After a time you work out how to operate the car and drive away, intrigued by all the gadgets, and marvelling at the speed with which you can travel between two points.

Once you settle into the leather seats, you are even more impressed to find that the car has yet another feature – a satellite linked computer mapping system that can help direct you to any point you desire. This is truly a marvellous machine.

As you use the vehicle more and more, day after day, you start to become accustomed to its features – you begin to take these features for granted. You start to look at other vehicles and you notice other features – alloy wheels, roofs that can retract, cruise control, and electronically controlled seat adjustments. You feel an urge to have these extra special features, and vow to save up to invest in these new technologies. You set yourself a goal to save up enough to purchase these extra features.

All the time, running on three, not four cylinders...

Table of Contents

Imagine that……..   7

Service is on the Decline   11
    The 'Cultural' Contribution   20

Does Culture 'Count'?   23
    The Cultural Complexity   27
    Examples of the Misunderstandings   30
    In a Nutshell   32

UGRs - Unlocking the Secrets of Corporate Culture   34
    The Tale of Five Monkeys   40
    Kick starting conversations that allude to UGRs   41
    The 'Smart Talk Trap' – What UGR is That?   46
    The Abilene Paradox – What UGR is That?   48
    The Saturn Story – What UGR is That?   49
    Examples of Other UGRs   51
    UGR Complexity   62
    Management UGRs   64
    Different UGRs in Different Organizational Types   69
    UGRs and Value Statements   71
    In a Nutshell   75

UGRs in a Different Context — 78
- A Goal is Scored — 79
- How Important is the Individual? — 80
- Time for Performance Review — 82
- The Australian Women's Field Hockey Team — 83
- The Chicago Bulls Basketball Team — 87
- The New Zealand Rugby Union Football Team — 91
- In a Nutshell — 95

How are UGRs established? — 98
- In a Nutshell — 104

Can UGRs Be Changed? — 105
- Indirect Cultural Change Methods — 106
- Direct Cultural Change Methods — 108
- The First Phase: Awareness — 110
- The Second Phase: Action — 111
- The Third Phase: Ongoing focus and follow up — 120
- Where to Start? — 124
- In a Nutshell — 127

UGRs Into the Future — 129
- Force #1 – The outcomes from an era of downsizing, mergers and acquisitions — 129
- Force #2 – The 'New Consumer' — 132
- Force #3 – The Internet and e-commerce — 135
- In a Nutshell — 138

UGRs – The Final View — 140

Appendix 1 — 145

UGRs at the XXX Organization — 145

Notes — 147

About the Author — 150

Service is on the Decline

When I read recent outcomes from the American Customer Satisfaction Index (ACSI), it confirmed exactly what I had been thinking for quite some time. Service is on the decline – everywhere.

The ACSI is a measure of customer satisfaction that is based on modelling of customer evaluations of the quality of goods and services that are purchased in the United States. The first ACSI was released in October 1994 and results have been released quarterly since that time.

The ACSI measures customer satisfaction with the goods and services of approximately 200 organizations, including seven government agencies. Organizations included in the survey are selected on the basis of their relative size within the industry sector. Government agencies selected for measurement are a small number of federal and local agencies with which a majority of household consumers can be expected to have had some recent first-hand contact and experience.

Analysis of changes in satisfaction over the 1994 – 2000 period show some fascinating trends, some of which are included in Table 1 below. Almost without exception, industry sectors are seeing a decline in customer satisfaction. Satisfaction with airlines has declined a staggering 12.5%, while satisfaction with services provided by motion picture companies has declined 11.7%.

Table 1:

American Customer Satisfaction Index scores, selected industries, 1994 and 2000, and percentage decline over that period

Selected Industries	1994	2000	% Change
PC industry	78	74	-5.1%
Airlines	72	63	-12.5%
Telecommunications*	75	72	-4.0%
Retail	75	73	-3.7%
Gas stations	80	75	-3.8%
Banks	74	70	-5.4%
Hotels	75	72	-4.0%
Hospitals	74	69	-6.8%

(*Baseline 1995)
(Source, American Customer Satisfaction Index, http://acsi.asq.org/, percentages rounded)

Service is on the Decline

The ACSI reports levels of customer satisfaction for each of the companies included in the survey. Table 2 below shows results for selected companies. Some of these results are remarkable as they show:

- Changes in levels of customer satisfaction with individual companies that do not necessarily reflect industry trends. I have included two computer companies to show that there was not a universal consumer backlash to the PC industry over the 1994-2000 period – as Dell Computer rated an increase in satisfaction of over 11%, while Compaq Computer Corporation scored a 9% decline in the same period

- Large declines in organizations that have in the past been seen as an icon for customer service. Southwest Airlines have been written about probably more than any other company in recent times – for their fun approach to service and their commitment to staff. Yet their customer satisfaction ratings declined by more than 10% over the period. Similarly, Nordstrom has been widely acknowledged as a model for companies to emulate in terms of its service ethic. Yet their customer satisfaction has declined by almost 10%

Table 2:

American Customer Satisfaction Index scores, selected companies, 1994 and 2000, and percentage decline over that period

Selected Companies	1994	2000	% Change
Dell Computer*	72	80	11.1%
Compaq Computer Corporation	78	71	-9.0%
Volkswagen of America, Inc.	74	83	12.2%
Delta Airlines	77	66	-14.3%
Southwest Airlines, Inc.	78	70	-10.3%
AT&T Corporation	85	75	-11.8%
Nordstrom, Inc	84	76	-9.5%
Kmart Corporation	74	67	-9.5%
First Union Corporation (Bank)	76	66	-13.2%
NIKE, Inc.	82	78	-4.9%

(*Baseline 1997) (Source, American Customer Satisfaction Index, http://acsi.asq.org/, percentages rounded)

A general dissatisfaction with service has been noted elsewhere around the world. In the 21st February 2001 edition the Straits Times – the major newspaper in Singapore – a headline read 'Poor service common here'. This article reported on more than 2000 complaints in three months to the Consumer Association of Singapore. These service related complaints were against a range of businesses, the most common of which were computer outlets, electronic goods stores, and furniture and home furnishing outlets. The article reports Prime Minister Goh Chok Tong having aired a view that the quality of service in Singapore did not match that of many countries he had visited.

This article was the catalyst for an avalanche of letters to the editor – the vast majority of which bemoaned the poor service by companies in Singapore. It also prompted another journalist to write another article in the 3rd March edition of the paper titled 'Rudeness? It's all part of the service'.

In the 19th October 2000 edition of the Australian newspaper, an article by Canadian journalist, James Deacon, celebrated the staging of the Sydney Olympics. After extolling the virtues of the organization of the games, and the hospitality of the locals, Deacon writes:

> 'Several newspaper columnists in the last days of the Games wondered in print when the real Sydney - apparently a crankier, less eager-to-please city than the one on display - would reassert itself.
>
> With a couple of days to explore once the Games ended, I kept an eye out.
>
> While shopping along Pitt Street, for instance, I went into three different stores looking for presents for my wife and kids. I also accompanied a friend who was trying to buy shoes at a sporting goods store. In three out of four stores, I would have had to set myself on fire to get any attention from staff. At the sporting goods store, my colleague, who would happily have spent $200 in a matter of minutes had someone just showed him around, simply walked away.

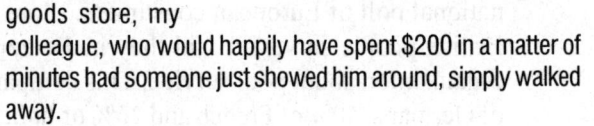

After 17 days of arena food, I booked tables at a couple of renowned restaurants. The meals were routinely excellent, and the settings sublime but the service was often slow and unreliable.

In a No Worries world, this is just quibbling. But after the Games, Sydney is no longer completely in a No Worries world. For three weeks, the Olympics were about sport but in the foreseeable future, the pay-off will be tourism.

The city dazzled 10,000 of the planet's broadcasters and writers, who extolled Sydney's virtues to an audience of billions, many of whom will now want to visit. And in the world's other great cities, tourists paying top dollar expect a commensurate level of service. That means service will either have to improve, or Sydneysiders who make their living off high-end tourism can expect some unhappy customers.'

One of the biggest outcries about service in Australia has been with regard to banks. In addition to concerns about the large number of branch closures, bank customers have become increasingly concerned about the de-personalisation of service provided by their financial institution. Technology driven call centres, increased fees and a drive by banks to promote customer use of electronic banking, have resulted in a massive backlash. In the 15th June 2000 edition of Business News, a Western Australian business newspaper, BankWest Managing Director Terry Budge is quoted as saying the anti-bank feeling in the community is worse than at any time during the 28 years of his involvement in the industry. 'I've never seen so much criticism of any industry', Mr Budge said.

An October 1998 BBC news release reports on an international poll of European consumers. More than half the British people surveyed said they had complained to an organization about poor service. This compares with 43% of Germans, 40% of French and 26% of Italians. UK firms were rated worst for customer service and are warned they must improve to compete with their international rivals. Companies in the United States give the best service to their customers, according to the survey (interestingly, the article did not refer to the ACSI!).

In the 1999 Zagat London Restaurant Survey with over 2500 respondents, 38% of them cited poor quality of service as their top irritant, as against 33% in the previous year's guide. Second gripe (30%) is the perennial moan about high prices. But service, 'from initial reservation to bill handling, is the area that most restaurateurs most need to address and improve' says Sholto Douglas-Home, Zagat's UK editor.

According to the China Economic Review, of the total of 93,010 complaints lodged by consumers in 60 cities across China during the first half of 2000, a record 46 per cent concerned services rather than products, according to a report by the State Administration for Industry and Commerce.

Against this backdrop of declining service satisfaction, a global customer backlash is now occuring. Customers are becoming more vocal about their concerns and there are now even web sites dedicated to naming companies that deliver poor service.

Notacceptable.com promotes itself as a free UK complaints web site. Its purpose is to:

- Assist individuals to obtain redress for complaints
- Find out what customers are complaining about
- Identify organizations with high complaint levels
- Identify organizations that don't deal effectively with valid complaints

Other web sites have been set up with the purpose of identifying organizations that provide 'good' and 'bad' service. Here are a few:

The Bad, Better and Best Bulletin Board - webBbox.com

As the site says 'Are you miffed by a product that doesn't work as advertised, and a manufacturer who doesn't seem to care? OR Are you thrilled with a company that is just delightful to do business with?'

AngryConsumer.Com

The 'home' page says it all:

'Am I the only angry consumer out there?

I don't think so. Here is the place to tell your story. Good things happen, too. We welcome both good and bad.'

thecomplaintstation.com

This site purports to hold the record for the most complaints of any one site. The purpose of The Complaint Station is to provide customers with a central location to file complaints or research previous complaints. You can request a complaint station be set up specific to a company or topic. 'Beware bad service providers!'

Bad Customer Service? - http://ourworld.cs.com/_ht_a/Robbienancyboyd/index.htm

This site has been created with a view to promoting organizations that provide good and bad service and for letting the world know about it! It is a place where you can say to the world, 'I went to this store, and do you know how I was treated?'

The Squeaky Wheel.com - http://www.thesqueakywheel.com/

'You don't have to put up with crummy products, broken promises or bad service anymore. Let us help you to get a refund today!' This site even compares its complaint features with other complaint sites to provide evidence that it is the best of the complaint sites!

Baddealings.com

Among other things, this site lists the 'top ten' companies that have been complained about.

Complaints.com

This site promotes itself as helping others avoid the same pitfalls that you have experienced. 'The entire world can read your complaints!'

eComplaints.com

eComplaints.com promotes itself to consumers as 'your chance to fight back'. The site highlights the point that the errant company will be exposed to fellow consumers. The site publishes the complaint on the web and a copy of the complaint is sent to the company.

In addition to these and other consumer complaint sites, a number of web sites are being developed specifically to target named businesses. For example, the site Untied.com is designed specifically as an ongoing record of poor service provided by United Airlines in the US.

The point in identifying these sites is that at a time when customers are increasingly dissatisfied with service, there are now more powerful and effective ways the negative sentiment can spread. Organizations providing poor service increasingly are at risk of losing business.

Paradoxically, many organizations have seen declining levels of customer satisfaction at the very same time as they have invested heavily into service improvements, including staff training, CRM systems, multiple and improved customer access points and the like. The question that looms large in these organizations is 'Why are we unable to arrest declining levels of satisfaction?'

The 'Cultural' Contribution

When referring to declining levels of customer satisfaction, I often get asked questions like these:

'But Steve, aren't service standards better than they used to be? Aren't most organizations providing better service?'

Of course, the inference behind these questions is right – in many cases, organizations have effected service improvements, yet their customers think less highly of them. In these cases, customer expectations have risen more quickly than their customers' perception of the quality of service. These expectations have increased as a consequence of higher levels of education, their experience with other organizations, and an increasing propensity to share concerns about poor service.

Consequently, one explanation for the service decline phenomenon is that customer expectations have risen more quickly than their perception of the quality of service delivery. But there is still something missing.

In my view, the service decline phenomenon has occurred primarily because of a lack of service culture. In the majority of organizations, if a culture of service pervades every level, every part of the company, it will follow that service will be delivered at or above customer expectations.

Intuitively, we all know this to be the case. We know that the culture of an organization is the foundation stone of service. Without a culture of service, related strategies will simply be cosmetic. With a culture of service, the possibilities are limitless.

Sadly, the culture of many organizations is not how we would want it.

The 'service decline' phenomenon is a symptom of much bigger issues that have affected businesses and governments over the past 15 years. In their 2000 book 'The New Corporate Cultures', Dean and Kennedy suggest that corporate cultures are in crisis because of a combination of events that include:

- The rise in shareholder value and 'short termism' – at the expense of customer service and employee loyalty
- Downsizing and re-engineering – culminating in employees realising that they must first look after 'number one'
- Outsourcing – and its implication that internal skills are not available or valuable
- Merger mania – and the effect of uncertainty of tenure that this has on people
- Computers and associated cultural isolation
- Globalisation – and the associated loss of the importance of local markets

These major developments have been potent forces working against strong and positive cultures. A key issue that needs to be considered relates to the impact of 'weak' cultures on the bottom line.

Does Culture 'Count'?

> Culture is one thing and varnish is another.
> Ralph Waldo Emerson, 1803-1882

Some of us have been lucky enough to experience a positive, healthy and upbeat culture, and again, common sense tells us this 'counts' in a positive way.

Research confirms this logic, and goes further still. In their book, 'Corporate Culture and Performance[1]', Kotter and Heskett make the following assertions:

- Corporate culture can have a significant impact on a firm's long term economic performance
- Corporate culture will probably be an even more important factor in determining the success or failure of firms in the next decade

- Corporate cultures that inhibit strong long term financial performance are not rare; they develop easily, even in firms that are full of reasonable and intelligent people

- Although tough to change, corporate cultures can be made more performance enhancing

It is worth pondering these propositions, as they have implications that are critical – this research tells us that culture counts, it is of increasing importance, that culture often is negatively oriented even in 'intelligent' organizations, and yet we can change it.

Writing some 20 years after their first book on corporate cultures, Deal and Kennedy in 'The New Corporate Cultures'[2] consider the question of whether or not strong organizational cultures pay off in financial performance. They report that in 1982, opinions were strongly divided on this issue. With the benefit of around 20 years hindsight, the picture has changed somewhat. In their 1982 book, 'Corporate Cultures: The Rites and Rituals of Corporate Life', Deal and Kennedy cite a number of companies as having strong, exemplary cultures. Not all of these companies have fared well in the ensuing years. Nonetheless, they report:

> 'Had we put our 1982 money where our mouths were and purchased one share of stock in each of the companies we so admired (which were then listed on the stock market), our initial stake would have increased by 987% through midyear 1998. In contrast, had we invested our money in the Standard and Poor's average, the most broadly based index of stock performance, our stake would have increased by only 538% - around half what we could have gained by betting on our exemplary companies.'

Deal and Kennedy go further in their analysis of the relationship between financial performance and corporate culture. They re-analysed data reported in a major study by Kotter and Heskett. Building on an analysis of the financial performance of 207 companies over an 11 year period, they report the following[3]:

- 'Culturally strong companies averaged 571% higher gains in operating earnings than those more culturally deprived over the same period
- Companies with highly rated cultures averaged 417% higher returns on investment than their less culturally robust counterparts
- Companies with strong cultures saw their stock price increase 363% more than their culturally challenged peers over the time span of the study'

The view that corporate culture is of critical importance to the success of a company is not confined to academic and business writers. In the April 28-29 2001 edition of the Australian Financial Review, Managing Directors of some of Australia's leading companies are interviewed in an article titled 'Keepers of the Corporate Soul'. When Paul

Anderson took over the then troubled BHP in 1998, most observers were quick to point out its highly internalised culture as a major problem he needed to fix. Anderson says corporate culture must first be established at the top, with quality leadership. When he first began, he spent hour long, one-on-one interviews with senior management to explain a new charter. The charter reads:

> 'Every employee starts each day with a sense of purpose and ends each day with a sense of accomplishment.'

It measures success according to how the communities in which BHP operates value their citizenship; how customers will benefit from services and products; and as shareholders enjoying superior returns.

Anderson says these values are a global model which must be transparent in foreign markets. Regular reports chart both problems and successes delivered to the communities in which BHP works.

Greg Mackay, an executive director with Macquarie Bank, describes how the culture works. 'We have a management philosophy which we call 'loose-tight'. There are a small number of very important things where we insist on tight conformity. Those are our values.

These goals are outlined in a booklet, 'What We Stand For', which nominates six principles: integrity, client commitment, strive for profitability, fulfilment for our people, teamwork and highest standards.'

> 'Everything else is in the 'loose' category,' Mackay says, 'which means we give a lot of discretion to people who are running particular operations. But always, underlying this, there are these universal standards.'

The bank's culture is high on CEO Allan Moss' agenda. 'I spend quite a lot of my week on that. I have lunch at least once a year with each of the top 20 per cent of the organization, in groups of 20-30. That's 800 people a year. We mostly talk about corporate culture. We talk about the six core values and how we should put these into practice.'

The Cultural Complexity

Edgar Schien recognised the importance of organizational culture in his 1992 book, 'Organizational Culture and Leadership'[4], when he said:

'There is a possibility, under-emphasised in leadership research, that the only thing of real importance that leaders do is to create and manage culture and that the unique talent of leaders is to work with culture'.

This is a very big call – particularly when, in my view, the concept of organizational culture has been very poorly understood in practical terms.

The concept of organizational culture has been around for a long time. When I completed my Masters degree in 1982, the term was not a new one then!

The problem is that the term 'organizational culture' has always had an academic and theoretical orientation. The various definitions and explanations of the term have not had a practical orientation, and have on many occasions contributed to a greater sense of impotence felt by managers. Indeed, in recent times I have made it a bit of a hobby to sift through texts that focus on corporate culture, and to locate the various definitions provided in these texts. Surprisingly, some authors fail to even try (a rather astonishing oversight when the term is part of the book title), while many others provide definitions that occupy pages.

As an example, Schein[5] sees organizational culture as:

> 'The pattern of basic assumptions which a group has invented, discovered or developed in learning to cope with its problems of external adaptation and internal integration.'

Writers in the marketing field provide a definition similar to that in organizational behaviour. Organizational culture is seen as:

> 'A pattern of shared values and beliefs that help individuals understand organizational functioning and thus provide them norms for behaviour in organizations.'[6]

Borgatti[7] provides a definition of the shared beliefs, values and norms that define a group's culture. They include:

> '• Cognitive schemas (Scripts and frames that mould our expectations and help us assign meaning and order to the stream of experience)
>
> • Shared meanings (Common interpretations of events)
>
> • Perceptions (How the world is, how things work. Implicit theories of the market, of management, of politics, of human nature)

- Prescriptions and Preferences (What the best way to do things is; What they want to happen)
- Behavioural codes (How to dress, how to act, what kinds of things you can joke about, is it OK to be late?)
- Basic values (What is really important; what is wrong or bad)
- Myths and legends (Stories about the past: knowledge of the stories identifies you as belonging, and often the stories have hidden points like 'this is what happens to people who...')
- Heroes and heroines
- Emblems (Objects that have meaning, like group t-shirts, gold watches)
- Rituals'

In creating a management awareness of organizational culture, many academics have created a monster. Management more and more have been aware of a counter-productive culture, or a less than optimum culture, but at the same time have felt powerless to tackle it.

This has been manifest in various forms. Many businesses have created impressive documents that make various proclamations about the importance of customers, staff, and the organizational commitment to these as the key priorities. Meanwhile, practice 'on the ground' can reflect almost the opposite.

As a result, the workforce culture is further entrenched in its negative orientation, as what staff read in corporate literature is known not to reflect reality. Cynicism builds, and the rhetoric - reality gap widens further.

Examples of the Misunderstandings

In a recent Australian journal dedicated to customer service[8], a feature article was run on organizational culture. The title of the article was 'How do you develop a service culture within your organization?' The article summarised interviews with four managers from different organizations. The content of the interviews is probably best described as a summary of useful *strategies* that each organization has deployed to 'develop the culture'. These *strategies* include:

- Customer service training sessions
- Regular meetings that deal with site conditions and customer needs
- Open problem solving
- Changing the focus of providing service to that of meeting the customers' business needs
- Assigning dedicated support professionals to the most valued customers
- The collection and analysis of detailed customer information
- The implementation of an effective system of measurement
- Awards and recognition for staff
- Developing a slogan such as 'people are our best property'
- Maintaining contact with the customer after the sale
- Clear job statements

This article is not alone in missing the point. People everywhere realise and argue the importance of a service culture, but they fail to grasp what 'organizational culture' really means. You see, the managers who were interviewed for this article identified a range of strategies that, in combination, they hoped would have a positive result on the organization's culture. But while managers search for the most useful tactics or strategies to implement to improve the culture, they are failing to address the core issue of corporate culture itself. It is my belief that this happens because people do not understand organizational culture in *practical* terms.

In my travels around different organizations, I consistently see evidence of people trying to develop a culture of service through the application of what they see as associated strategies. Many organizations attempt to do this through the creation of vision and mission statements, values statements, and the like[9].

All these visions, missions and values begin to look alike, irrespective of the organization's size or industry sector. A vision statement in one organization could, on many occasions, be imported into another organization. 'Values' statements start to look the same across most organizations. Perhaps even worse, often the language contained within these is alienating and remote for the majority of staff. As an example, consider the following 'values', which are the first three from a much longer list of values contained in a staff document in a major Australian company:

- We will honour all commitments to our customers, employees and shareholders
- We will conduct our business with unwavering high standards of honesty, trust, professionalism and ethical behaviour

- We will communicate openly and frequently with all constituents with a principle of communicating what we know, when we know it

No one can argue against intentions behind these values, but I would argue that few people in this organization would *really* know and commit to these. Value statements like these sound bureaucratic and a little autocratic, and as a 'stand alone' might make the management feel good, but have very little impact on staff. Indeed, I would like to approach staff in this organization at random and ask them if they actually knew what was written in this document. I think I know what the answer would be.

In a Nutshell

- We all know, intuitively, that a positive culture makes a big difference to how much we give at work

- Research has confirmed our implicit understandings about corporate culture – in a large study of companies over an 11 year period, corporations with a strong culture substantially outperformed other companies in many ways, including their operating earnings, returns on investment and their stock prices

- Some CEOs of large companies have begun to realise that establishing the right culture is a prerequisite for improved business performance

- Academics and other business writers have not provided much in practical terms for managers to 'manage' their culture. Most definitions of organizational culture are lengthy, abstract and

Does Culture 'Count'

difficult to translate into actions a manager might deploy

- Many managers now know about the importance of corporate culture, and attempt to improve it by implementing service-related tactics and strategies that they hope by osmosis will improve the work culture
- Many Values Statements, which are intended to shape corporate culture, have been established by a small group of senior people, and are framed in terms that are bureaucratic and autocratic

UGRs® - Unlocking the Secrets of Corporate Culture

> Culture is a little like dropping an Alka-Seltzer into a glass — you don't see it, but somehow it does something. Hans Magnus Enzensberger

'In a growing number of companies, 'team players' are seen as those whose car is first into the car park each morning and last to leave at night. In one company a senior manager walks around the car park at 7.30 am and feels the radiator in every vehicle – those still warm earn a black mark on the personnel file of the owners.

In a work world where the fear of being overtaken by ambitious colleagues keeps many chained to their desks, acts of deception are practiced that in a less fraught context would seem laughably childish. Some US office workers for example, advance the times shown on their emails before surreptitiously leaving by a rear entrance. One New York banking executive is reported to bribe security guards with hot stock tips in return for their looking the other way as he creeps from the building around 7.30 each evening.'[10]

When I first came across the concept of corporate culture in 1982, it was of passing interest. Although I saw the inherent logic underpinning the concept, I felt confused as to what could be done in practical terms to influence it.

I guess I saw a corporate culture as a 'given' that could not be changed.

That view remained until I heard a presentation from a manager of McDonalds. This manager used a term that changed my conception of corporate culture[11]. The term he used was simple, yet powerful. He said:

'At McDonalds, this is the way we do things around here'.

While that may not be too shattering for you, it was for me! From my perspective, the connections were finally made - the concept of corporate culture finally made sense.

I reflected on the fact that McDonalds employ teenagers - an age group commonly recognised as the most rebellious and resistant to authority. At the same time, McDonalds have a reputation worldwide for consistency. Whether or not one liked the McDonalds product, they were achieving something with their staff through this worldwide consistency!

This is when I derived a new term - a term that I think goes a long way to clarifying corporate culture. **The term I conceived was Unwritten Ground Rules, or 'UGRs®'**.

The best way to acquire an understanding of UGRs is to consider actual UGRs in an organization that I am aware of. This organization's UGRs were as follows:

- At our meetings it isn't worth complaining because nothing will get done
- The only time anyone gets spoken to by the boss is when something is wrong
- The company talks about good customer service, but we know they don't really mean it, so we don't really have to worry about it
- Our funniest jokes usually involve making jokes about our work colleagues
- We go through the motions with our bosses, once they've gone we do what we want

When I first share these during presentations, I often get a sense from at least part of the audience that they feel slightly uneasy. My hunch is that these UGRs are so close to the mark that at least some people begin to feel uncomfortable.

Some people are even brave enough to comment 'Have you been watching us?'

It is worth considering for one moment an organization that has comprehensive and attractively presented documentation to support its operations. This documentation may cover policies, procedures, job descriptions, and customer service standards. The organization may even have an impressive Customer Service Charter. It may even have all procedural documentation relevant for conformance to international quality standards. A question worth asking is 'Which counts most – the documentation or the UGRs?'

In my view, there is nothing more powerful in an organization than its UGRs. If 'happy' staff in any given organization talked about why they were happy at their work, I guarantee many reasons would relate to positive UGRs. Similarly, if 'unhappy' staff in an organization talked about why they were unhappy at their work, I guarantee many reasons for being unhappy would relate to the UGRs.

The incredible feature of UGRs is that they hold so much power, yet they are rarely talked about.

An excellent test for UGRs in an organization is a relatively new employee. When a new employee begins at an organization, they will probably be given an induction or orientation. At this orientation or induction they are told 'This is the way we do things around here...' Then they go and find out the truth - and they find out by deduction.

New employees watch for the subtle and not-so-subtle cues as to 'how we do things around here'. They quickly learn about acceptable and accepted practices within the organization by watching and listening.

The specific events where people deduce UGRs are many and varied, but they include:

- If and how staff talk to one another
- How staff talk to customers
- What staff say about a customer when the telephone is put down
- How staff talk when a manager is present, and what they say when that person walks away
- What is said in staff rooms
- What is talked about in the corridors immediately *after* a meeting
- How a different point of view is handled within meetings, and whether the person with this different viewpoint is valued or isolated

- Whether people are encouraged to share their views
- Whether people laugh, and what they laugh at (or who they laugh at, or about)

UGRs have incredible power over people. Anyone who has tried to fight against a UGR knows how difficult a job it is.

When I first entered the workforce as a young teacher, I worked in a school where the UGRs were:

- Isolation is king - people stay away from the staff room
- Parents are to be treated with the deepest suspicion
- School is to be evacuated by 3.30
- Staff meetings are for one-way information dissemination and discussion of problem students (who behave these ways because of incompetent teachers)
- We treat children differently when parents are around

From the outside (or 'on the surface') this was a quiet, efficient and functional school!

The next school I was transferred to was in country Western Australia. This school had a mix of older staff who had been at the school for a number of years, and younger staff who were in the early part of their teaching careers. I discovered very quickly that the UGRs were extremely powerful and included:

- The social well being of staff is extremely important, so we joke, laugh and socialise a lot
- The leadership team has exclusivity in so far as *you* are able to relate to their style of humour and their

'inside' stories (the emphasis here is intended to convey the point that *you* had to conform)

- A sign of being included as part of the 'leader group' is being invited to play golf
- The only time students are talked about in the staff room is when they have done something we can laugh about
- 'Rank' and 'status' come from experience and time served at the school, and bring privileges that are discussed and organised away from the view of others

Again from the outside, this was a positive, happy school! As I reflect on it now, I feel for some of the younger female teachers in particular, who were not extroverts, and who were unable to gain access to the inner sanctum. They must have had a very lonely existence during work hours.

As a younger man, working to pay for my university degree, I worked as a casual employee with a furniture removal company. I was one of many 'jockeys' – the young men who accompany the older drivers to lift the other end of heavier furniture. I can still remember the catch cry of many of the drivers with whom I worked - 'Mine is not to wonder why, mine is just to do or die'. What a UGR that was - as workers, we just do what we're told - the thinking is left to management!

During times when business was not as brisk, there was a UGR in this company that staff must look busy when 'senior' bosses were around. It was OK to relax when they were not around, but we were to be ever vigilant in case they made a surprise entry. Another UGR related to the relationship between us younger men as 'jockeys' and the older drivers. The UGR here was NEVER question the judgement of a driver. Better to stay quiet than to point out a potential weakness in the judgement of a driver, particularly when others were around.

These same drivers would treat us jockeys with complete respect when customers or bosses were around. Alone, or in front of other drivers, our treatment differed dramatically. Reflecting on this, there was probably a UGR among drivers that said:

Around here, if you display compassion to younger 'jockeys' you display an inherent weakness in your character, which will exclude you from the driver group.

Anyone who doubts the power of UGRs should reflect on what is purported to be a true story about an experiment conducted by behavioural scientists.

The Tale of Five Monkeys

Behavioural scientists are said to place five monkeys in a cage. In the cage is a ladder, and at the top of the ladder is a bunch of bananas. The cage is a normal cage, except for the fact that it has sprinklers in the ceiling through which water can flow.

Not long after being placed in the cage, the monkeys spot the bananas. They begin their climb up the ladder, and the behavioural scientists press a switch that turns on the sprinklers. The monkeys get drenched.

The monkeys try again, and the same happens. The sprinklers are turned on and they get drenched.

This happens again and again. Eventually the monkeys give up trying to get the bananas.

> The scientists then remove one of the monkeys and put a new one into the cage. The new one spots the bananas and naturally begins to climb the ladder. A fascinating thing happens. The other monkeys aggressively jump on the new monkey and pull it down. The new monkey tries again, and again it gets set upon. Again it tries - the same consequence. Eventually the new monkey ceases trying.
>
> The scientists then take another of the original monkeys out and replace it with a new one. The new monkey tries to climb the ladder and it is set upon. This happens time and again, until the newest of the monkeys stops trying to climb the ladder.
>
> Eventually each of the original monkeys is replaced.
>
> The scientists then place another new monkey in the cage and it is jumped on aggressively and pulled down by the other monkeys.
>
> Why? Not one of them knows…

This story highlights the power of UGRs. Anyone who has tried to change a UGR knows that they are often not too subtly 'dragged down' by others. UGRs have enormous power to control our behaviour.

Incredibly, they are rarely talked about openly.

Kick starting conversations that allude to UGRs

Normal work conversations are most often based on information exchange about day-to-day work, business competitors, and internal and external customers. This is the routine aspect of work that is focussed primarily on getting things done, and on overcoming simple day-to-day problems.

From time to time, given the right context, conversations breach the norm and cross into UGR related discussions. The right context is imperative here – and this normally means the 'right' people being together in a setting that has privacy, and without the presence of specific people. One person – the initiator - will give a specific cue to invite a discussion that relates to one or more UGRs. Signals from the UGR conversation initiator include questions like:

- So what's the *real* story about Barry's transfer to another section?
- Did you hear what I heard about Janet?
- Did you see how John reacted when Mary spoke up at the meeting?

This is a beginning cue that the initiator is willing to engage in a discussion on information not necessarily known by the receiver. Alternatively, the initiator has sufficient trust with the receiver that they are willing to confirm their own understanding of a UGR – safe in the knowledge that the receiver will not use the information against him or her. It is expected that once this conversation is responded to, the initiator will also get something in response. In essence the conversation is horse-trading of information not known about by the other party. It fosters and promotes UGRs.

The following example of this is based around a UGR which is:

Around here it isn't worth complaining because we know that nothing will get done.

Initiator: "Could you believe Barry (the boss) in that meeting when he asked if there were any concerns about the decision to change our marketing approach? (This is the invitation to begin discussion about the UGR.)"

Responder: "As if he actually expected someone to answer. Does he think we're all fools, or is he really so blind that he can't see what's happened in past meetings. Every single suggestion we've had in the past has been greeted with a big fat nothing."

Initiator: "No way – he's not blind. He is acutely aware of what he's doing. He's covering his backside. When this new marketing approach doesn't work, he'll argue that it wasn't his fault. He'll say he gave all of us the opportunity to respond. He's not dumb – he's just a nasty political animal. The problem is, none of the bosses above him are any different. They all go through the motions, 'act' as though they're listening to us, then go ahead and do whatever they intended to do in the first place."

Responder: "You're not wrong – did you hear what Janet did last week..."

At this point in the discussion, another person comes into the room where this discussion has been taking place. This person is relatively new to the organization, but has demonstrated that they are relatively trustworthy.

Meeting newcomer: "Hi guys – hope I'm not interrupting something here?"

Initiator: "No problem, we're just catching up on the local gossip."

Meeting newcomer: "Actually, I'm glad I've caught up with both of you. I was going to get your advice on next week's meeting. You see, I've been thinking about this new marketing approach that's been proposed, and I think there are some serious flaws, that could result in some fairly negative repercussions. I know the decision has been made, but I was thinking of raising my concerns at the meeting."

Initiator: "Ah, how do I put this? You would be making a big mistake by doing this. You see, what's really happening here is..."

In this discussion, the UGR has been ratified and reinforced by the two initial players. They confirmed with each other that nothing will get done from complaints. When the newer staff member enters the discussion, a UGR lesson is about to take place. With the words 'You see, what's really happening here is...', the new staff members is about to learn the UGR. Unless the new staff member is extremely strong, he/she will conform.

Interestingly, discussions that allude to UGRs can also take place in large group situations. These tend to be much shorter, and are often backhanded comments that are negatively focussed.

I see and hear this constantly in seminars that I run, particularly when the participants are from the same organization and sufficient trust has been built within the group. Examples include:

- Steve, do you realise what the management of this organization is like?
- When is management going to get exposed to this kind of thinking? It's all very fine for us to hear this, but what about the management?
- I've learned that you're better off in this place to keep your head low, and say nothing

UGRs can be reinforced in public sessions even when the management is present. An example of this is a typical training seminar or in-house briefing where one or more of the managers make a presentation to staff. During a presentation, one of the managers begins a discussion:

Manager: "Our vision for the coming year is an exciting one. We recognise the problems that you have faced over the past 12 months – particularly when it comes to the budgetary pressures you have been placed under. This year however, heralds a new approach. As a management team, we plan to change the way we work with you, and to have an orientation on support, rather than pressure."

Mumbled, but clear enough for a number of the audience to hear, comes a comment "Well, well, this is the very first time we've heard this. And pigs can fly as well..."

A number of smiles appear, and faces turn to look at the person who has made the comment.

And from another part of the room "Good, can I now have the increase in budget I asked for."

Again, a number of smiles and heads turn.

Manager: "This time we are serious. I know things have been tough in the past, but we are really keen to re-build bridges, and to give you support to achieve your business goals..."

In this case there are clear UGRs that state:

- Around here, the management do a lot of talking, but more often than not the talk is not followed by action
- Around here, the only time we will believe management is when we actually see results from what they've talked about
- Around here, we can't trust management

45

- Around here, cynicism is OK (this is a particularly interesting UGR that the management have indirectly reinforced, through their acceptance of the cynical comments)

As I have dug further into the issues associated with UGRs, it has become more and more apparent that they underpin just about every aspect of our work.

As an example, in my readings lately, I have come across three fascinating pieces of work that shed a great deal of light on aspects of leadership and teamwork in business settings. These are:

- The Smart Talk Trap, raised in a recent edition of the Harvard Business Review, and a topic that is the subject of a recently published book
- The Abilene Paradox, a 'not so recent' insight into group dynamics
- The Saturn Story, a company created with a very different mindset

On thinking through each of these, I am convinced that they are underpinned by powerful UGRs.

The 'Smart Talk Trap' – What UGR is That?

In the May/June 1999 edition of the Harvard Business Review[12], there is an excellent article by Jeffrey Pfeffer and Robert Sutton called 'The Smart-Talk Trap'.

In this article the authors describe a phenomenon they have observed and researched in organizations of all sizes and types. They conclude that in many organizations an inhibitor of action is the 'Smart Talk Trap'. It is proposed that many organizations deal with problems by having a series of meetings. In these meetings, credence is given to those who are articulate and confident. Often these people are negatively oriented, and talk in abstract, complex terms. The outcomes from discussions lead by these people is either criticism for criticism's sake, or confusion.

It is claimed that these same people are often short on action – that this talk is a substitute for action. Interestingly, what gets rewarded in these organizations is normally not linked to actions. These organizations reward those who can engage in 'smart talk', and the capacity to exhibit this skill becomes an end in itself.

This is a fascinating observation that is clearly underpinned by one or more UGRs that could be as follows:

- Around here, if you are able to sound impressive in front of those who count, then you are held in high esteem. Actions and outcomes are not important

- Around here, you never want to expose your weaknesses, as this could be used against you in the future. One way to expose a weakness is by admitting that you don't understand what somebody else said

- The more sophisticated we sound, the more attention we get. The more attention we get, the more rewards

The Abilene Paradox – What UGR is That?

In his 1988 book, Professor Jerry Harvey of George Washington University[13] developed a parable of real life to describe how people believe they have reached agreement.

The story is about four adults - a married couple and the wife's parents – who are relaxing on a porch in 104 degree heat in the small town of Coleman, Texas, around 53 miles from Abilene. They are relaxing, drinking lemonade, and occasionally playing the game of dominoes.

The wife's father suggests they drive to Abilene to eat at the cafeteria. While the son in law thinks the idea is a crazy one, he goes along with it, as do the two women. They get in their car, which does not have air conditioning, and drive through a dust storm to Abilene. They eat a mediocre lunch and return to Coleman exhausted, hot, and generally unhappy with the experience.

When they are home, it is revealed that *none* of them wanted to go to Abilene. Each of them was going along because they thought the others wanted to go.

Again, this is a fascinating parable that illustrates UGRs that commonly exist in work environments. Translated into a work context, the following UGRs could be operating:

- Around here, positive group dynamics are most important. Anyone who disagrees does not have the group's best interests at heart, and is trying to ruin positive group dynamics

- Around here, if the boss wants something done, it's best not to disagree

- Around here, action – *any* action – is better than nothing

The Saturn Story – What UGR is That?

In 1985, General Motors established a separate and new division called Saturn. Set up with a view to creating a company that was markedly different in its operational style in the industry, and in the relationship it was to have with its customers, the division's philosophy was created by a committee of 99 people (originally there were 100, equally divided between union and management, but one resigned). After studying successful companies in other industries, recruiting and training staff, the division made its first car in 1990.

Made up almost exclusively of people from General Motors, Saturn set itself apart in many ways, including its mission statement, which is to:

> 'Market vehicles developed and manufactured in the United States that are world leaders in quality, cost and customer enthusiasm through the integration of people, technology and business systems and to exchange knowledge, technology and experience throughout General Motors.'

The company had an exhaustive recruitment process aimed at achieving 'cultural fit'.

> 'Seniority (at General Motors) had no meaning in the Saturn environment. So, no matter how long you had worked for GM, it was a share of the pain, share the gain, and everybody was going to work the same working hours. They knew there would be rotational shifts… The application (for a job at Saturn) was an eight page document that was every bit as detailed as a college application would be… We did paper and pencil testing. We did groups skills assessment… They went

through a two day screening process, at the end of which they got a job offer, or they didn't.'[14]

Overlaid on this different philosophy was a management structure that was as flat as could be, and a communication system that encouraged worker input at every point. These early, and subsequent efforts at Saturn have paid off – the company has a world-class record in employee retention. Other measures also point to the company being distinctly different in the automobile industry – the company has had good sales, it enjoys an excellent reputation and has a constructive, action-orientated, proud culture.

In more recent years there has been a push by General Motors for staff and management from Saturn to integrate into the rest of the company, so that the Saturn learnings can flow through the parent company. After spending some time in Saturn then being placed in a more traditional part of General Motors, manager Anna Kretz commented:

> 'I remember when I left Saturn, probably within the first six months someone called me, and said, 'Well, what have you been able to implement in your new job that you learned at Saturn?' And I'll never forget that question because the answer was, 'Nothing'... There needs to be enough people sufficient to cause momentum... There are some fundamental beliefs you have to share with a group of people. And if you don't have those fundamental beliefs then the rest of the stuff – the little things – have nothing to hang onto, so they don't become as meaningful to implement on an individual basis.'[15]

This is a stark example of strong UGRs in force. What Kretz was a victim of, but was unable to articulate, was a set of powerful UGRs that prevented her from gaining support for her ideas. With knowledge of the situation only as an outsider, I would hazard a guess that some of the prevailing UGRs she encountered on her return to General Motors, may have included these:

- Around here, we value ideas that *we* generate
- Around here, plenty of people come in from the outside with great ideas, but they don't really understand our business – we're different
- Around here, 'outsiders' can expose our limited creativity, so we avoid them and their ideas as much as possible
- Around here, if you stall for long enough on 'outside' people's ideas, they will stop trying to push them

Further, I would guess at a more specific UGR at General Motors that might be something like this:

Around here, it's fine for Saturn people to come in and try to implement their ideas, but their context is different. They hand-picked their staff – we didn't. The Saturn outsiders need to live in the real world.

Examples of Other UGRs

It is not hard to find UGRs in operation within any team. All of us have experienced them, and most of us have conformed. Some other UGRs that I have experienced are as follows:

The only way you learn about the range of entitlements to staff benefits is through serving time and asking the right questions

When I first entered head office of the Education Department after completing my Masters Degree, I was overwhelmed by the way in which the bureaucracy operated.

There was a level of clinical formality that I had never experienced before, and I was left to my own devices to 'survive'.

In the early to mid 1980s, this was the public service at its prime. There was no induction or orientation, the dress codes were extremely strong (although not explicit), and there were well defined territorial boundaries that meant different sections did not fraternise with other sections.

If you wanted to know something, you had to ask. Information was never offered in a proactive sense – you had to *think of the right question*, then *find the right person*. If you did not ask the right person, then you could not find the right answer. Importantly, the right person had to have two qualities – they had to know the right answer, and they had to be willing to share that information with you. With either of these conditions not satisfied, you could not get the right answer. I came to the conclusion after a short time that there was a direct correlation between the time people had spent in central office, and their willingness to divulge information. In essence, the longer a person had been in the building, the less willing they were to share.

I am not talking about the sharing of information on major organizational policies here – I am talking about some of the most basic of needs. These information needs included how you got extra suspension files for your filing cabinet, how you organised for large photocopy jobs, your leave entitlements, whether you were permitted to use the telephone for personal calls, how to get pens and paper (I am serious here!) and so on.

A bigger issue related to parking your car. After a time, I noticed that all of my work colleagues parked their car under the building. I competed with hundreds of others to find a parking space outside – and often in the extremely hot sun, or on a wet and windy day. Only after I had generated a degree of rapport did I summon up courage to ask one of my colleagues about whether I might be able to get a car park under the building. The answer given was a mumbled attempt at explaining that there were no spaces available.

After one full year, I learned that some of my colleagues were cheating the parking system. During a social function one Friday evening, and probably because some members of the team were suitably imbibed, I was finally accepted and let 'in' on the deal. I was told how I too could cheat the system.

Keep quiet in meetings and you do not get extra jobs

This UGR is incredibly powerful, and comes from the viewpoint that people who speak up are 'landed with jobs'. This UGR is still alive and well in many teams right now.

Most of us have seen it happen – a new staff member enters the team with enthusiasm. At meetings they offer an idea, and the group agrees that the idea is a good one. The manager then encourages the new staff member to take the idea to the next step, and staff members look at each other with a subtle wry grin – confirming the UGR that good ideas mean more work. This wry grin also is a signal between people that each of them knows the UGR and each of them has once again played the game correctly.

Ideas on innovation and change are welcomed as long as they do not require extra money

This UGR emerges after staff have been informed on a number of occasions that 'the resources don't exist to do this, even though we know it's needed'. In this situation, staff can see the need for an improvement, but management is not able to respond because of financial constraints.

These same managers are often heard to say to the staff 'We value and need your ideas...'

I have seen this UGR emerge where there are scarce resources for the front line staff, but where managers are seen to take receipt of their new company vehicle, or where managers are away for two weeks on an overseas 'business trip'.

Personal actions are selected on the basis of whether or not they will impact positively on career advancement

I first observed this UGR when I was involved in a major change programme in a large organization. The change programme involved the possibility of staff losing their jobs, and I saw personalities change!

I saw a number of staff lose sight of their day-to-day job, and begin the game of internal politics. Their productivity declined to almost zero, and their actions centred solely on career survival and advancement. One to one and small group meetings could be seen taking place everywhere. There was a clear delineation of whether or not you were of any 'career advancement value' to these people, and if you were not, you did not figure in any of their conversations.

After sufficient numbers of staff demonstrated these behaviours, this new UGR emerged - personal actions are selected on the basis of whether or not they will impact positively on career advancement. If you were not engaging in these secret meetings, you felt as though you were 'on the outside'.

Staff seen as 'good' by management are given more opportunities to display their talents, thereby reinforcing the already positive bias

This UGR is an interesting one that can emerge without management knowing what they are doing. Again I can reflect back to a time when I was working in a large team in a large organization.

From time to time, we could see one or two members of the team meeting with the manager, in the manager's office behind a closed door. At the next staff meeting, there would be an announcement that 'Mary and John' had agreed to take on this new project. It just so happened that 'Mary and John' were perceived as being on-side with the management, and therefore were more likely to get the 'good' jobs, where they could further display their skills.

I can still remember other staff engaging in discussions about the process that lead to 'Mary and John' being allocated that job. There was a strong sense of unfairness about that process, and the UGR was strengthened.

An individual's standing is related to how they relate in a social context with senior management

I have sometimes wondered whether studies on organizational behaviour have ever centred on the social aspect of work relationships. In my experiences, there is a clear distinction between work groups and *social* work groups, with there being a distinct advantage from the latter. I have sensed a strong UGR in many teams that says 'If you socialise with management, you have a clear run on the issues, you have higher standing, and you will ultimately be better off'.

An individual's value is measured by the hours they spend at work – and whether they are prepared to remain after normal work hours

In his book 'Maverick'[16], Ricardo Semler talks about the wholesale and radical changes he implemented when he took over his father's company, Semco, a Brazilian manufacturing organization. Semco is now regarded as a world leader in the industry. One of the observations he made when he took over the company was that people's performance was judged largely on the number of hours they spent at the desk. Staff who arrived early and left late must have been good!

There is an interesting spin on this UGR if the managers also spend long hours in their office. I have seen cases where the staff working long hours have gained access to these managers either very early in the morning, or very late in the evening. In these situations, the manager is often less formal (it is outside normal work hours), so there is a greater likelihood that the manager will share information that would not be otherwise shared.

In my travels around different organizations, I have seen a different slant on this UGR in action. In cases where people are unable to stay after normal work hours, I have literally heard comments alluding to whether or not that staff member is really committed to the organization, or to the team.

In one case when I was consulting with a team that was experiencing severe morale problems, a staff member indicated they would be unable to attend a social function. This function was organised by some of the other staff for the specific purpose of improving the sense of teamwork in the unit. Staff were quite angry at this individual, who in their eyes was once more displaying a lack of commitment to the team. I found out later that this person had to be home to care for her dying father, and for her own personal reasons, she wanted this kept confidential.

Part time staff are not 'real' staff

In a workforce that is now configured with a higher proportion of part time staff, this UGR is particularly dangerous. I have seen this UGR in operation when the full time staff feel as though they are a unit, supplemented by the part time staff. Part time staff are not involved in the same number of meetings held with full time staff, they tend to work more 'by the clock', so they are supplementary staff who do not 'count as much'.

Contract staff can be given the worst jobs, as they are least likely to complain

In an organization that has a mix of permanent and temporary staff, I was informed that more than one of the managers gave the temporary staff the worst jobs as they were least likely to complain. According to my sources, if the temporary staff member wanted a job in the future, they would need to comply with the boss' request, because the boss could easily find alternative temporary staff.

In one organization, the manager had made this explicit to the temporary staff member, who dared to question the allocation of her work duties. In response to the question from the temporary staff, the manager asked – 'Do you want work with us next year or not?'

Opposing views are a personal attack

This UGR is prominent in cases where people or groups are ill equipped to handle negative feedback. We have all been in situations where an individual or group actually says 'Please give us your feedback – we value the opportunity to improve'. When this UGR is at work, negative feedback is regarded as a personal attack, and we quickly learn that it is not worth our while engaging in this type of feedback again.

The signs that a person does not want to hear negative feedback range from the very subtle to the not so subtle, but most of us very easily get the message.

Once this happens, it does not matter how many times the individual or group mouths the words 'Your feedback is important, and we really value it'. The UGR is established, and it will take a lot to change it.

Being honest and open scars you for life, particularly if it relates in a negative way towards senior management

This is a UGR that is prominent for those people who have been with an organization for a longer period of time, and who have seen people suffer from being honest. The senior management may have professed to be open to feedback (as per the previous UGR – 'Opposing views are a personal attack') but when confronted with the 'truth' have been unable to accept it. If the person or people who have shared their views subsequently encounter a negative experience (transfer, non selection for promotion etc.), then two and two are put together.

This UGR is prominent in autocratically managed teams, where fear of reprisals is the main motivating factor. It is also prominent in organizations where there is a façade of friendliness, but where the management execute strong actions without consultation.

We do not tell the management about opportunities to improve the business, as it will only work against us

Recently when I was making a presentation to a group of people from different organizations, a gentleman asked whether his courier business was operating under the influence of a negative UGR. The situation is as follows:

The couriers in this company are very busy and from time to time they realise that they have deliveries that cause them to overlap territories. These couriers have worked out that if they swap mail they can be more efficient in two respects:

- It saves them time and allows them to complete their day faster than they otherwise would
- The customers get their deliveries quicker

This efficiency is not communicated to the management however. If the management become aware of the time saved by the couriers their pay is reduced relative to the amount of time they save. If they save half an hour, their pay gets docked by half an hour.

A new employee's enthusiasm will only be short lived – after a couple of months, they will learn that there is little to get excited about

This is an unusual UGR in so far as it is probably the most commonly verbalised of all UGRs. When a new employee takes up their position, their excitement and enthusiasm for the job is often evident. At meetings, they may offer ideas on how things could be improved, and they may offer to take on new work assignments. When this UGR is in force, more long standing staff will look at each other with a 'knowing smirk' on their faces. Out of earshot of the new staff, the comment 'Give him two months' will typically be made.

A new staff member is to be treated with the deepest suspicion, and must earn their stripes before being accepted as part of the 'inside' group

This UGR is particularly evident in work teams where there is already a strong team bond. The experiences and common understandings that keep a team together often have the simultaneous effect of shielding others from entry into the team.

In the eyes of existing team members, new staff need to earn their stripes before they can be seriously considered as part of the team. To earn their stripes, they must first demonstrate their:

- Intellectual capacities (being too different is the key issue here)
- Personality type
- Reactions to other staff and the management (whose side are they *really* on when it comes to a difficult situation)
- Social tendencies

If there is a fair degree of affinity across all these areas, then entry into the team is granted. Naturally, this takes time.

New staff are not informed about critical UGRs until they have earned their stripes. They earn their stripes by showing that they are capable of deducing the most important UGRs

During the intervening period between appointment to a position, and acceptance as part of the team, the new staff member is being judged by management and colleagues (the same applies if the new appointee is at management level). During this judgement period, the existing team will observe and rate how the new staff member copes in various situations and whether or not they are able to conform to existing practices.

If there are tensions between staff and management, the staff will also make judgements to establish whose 'side' the new appointee is on. This is determined through a variety of tests that include:

- Whether or not the new appointee parrots the proclamations made by senior management
- Whether the new staff member makes enquiries as to what is 'really' going on
- The extent to which the new staff member supports other staff in the presence of management (or dares to put colleagues down in front of management)
- The extent to which the new appointee talks rather than listens (this is a particularly important cue)
- The extent to which the new staff member says words to the effect 'Well, back in my previous company, what we did was ......' (the more this is used, the worse off the individual[17])

Based on the collective judgements of the team, the new appointee will be granted a level of entry into the team. These 'levels' range from being sustained as a relative outsider, through to being central to the team's gossip mongering, and the UGRs.

This process of staff scrutiny of new appointees has given rise to another concept that I have called the *'Propensity to be UGR-smart'*. It follows that if staff are being judged on their behaviours as described above, then some new appointees are bound to be 'smarter' than others in assessing the prevailing UGRs and acting accordingly.

Some staff are more 'UGR perceptive' than other staff and have an ability to deduce prevailing UGRs when they join an organization. These UGR-smart staff will have an instant advantage over other new staff, and have the capacity to work the system and progress through the ranks. That is of course conditional upon them playing the game according to the UGRs.

UGR-dumb staff on the other hand, are doomed from the start. These people, through their inability or unwillingness to grasp the prevailing UGRs, will constantly battle to remain, and will ultimately lose the battle unless they conform.

UGR Complexity

Because UGRs are people's perceptions of 'the way we do things around here', there is a tangled network of UGRs within even small work groups. They exist at various levels that include:

- Staff UGRs that are related to their close colleagues, other staff, and other sections/departments
- Staff UGRs about middle and senior management
- Staff UGRs about customers

In any organization, there will be varying levels of UGR concordance among staff. It may be that there is universal agreement among staff on the majority of UGRs. Equally, there may be widely different views on UGRs, even within the same sections of a company.

As an example, some staff within a section may be bound by a UGR that says:

Around here, the only reason staff go beyond the call of duty is to impress the boss

The staff who perceive this to be a UGR may have been in the business for a number of years, and may have worked extra hard for no reward or recognition. They may also hold the view that their managers have unfairly become closer to other staff who have done that little bit extra.

Other staff in the same section may be bound by a contradictory UGR that says:

Around here, doing that little bit extra is encouraged and recognised

In cases where there are relatively uniform UGRs, it fair to say there is a 'strong' culture in place. In cases where there are conflicting, or contrasting UGRs, it is reasonable to conclude there is a 'weak' culture. It is worth noting that a 'strong' culture is not necessarily a positive attribute – as there may be a set of uniformly negative UGRs in place. If this were the case, it would prove a much more time-consuming process to change the culture to a more positive orientation.

Management UGRs

To date, I have referred mainly to UGRs as they are perceived by staff. However, just as staff are bound by their UGRs, so too are managers. Again there is a complex mix of UGRs held by managers that include:

- Management UGRs about their close colleagues, other managers and other sections/departments
- Management UGRs about staff
- Management UGRs about customers

In the section that follows, I give details of some of the management related UGRs that I have come across in recent years. The first set relates to *management UGRs about close colleagues, other managers and other sections/departments.*

We keep our cards close to our chest to protect and build our empires, and to avoid the risk of our weaknesses being exposed

Empire building is a prominent goal in organizations where there is little trust. Typically, this UGR is strong soon after a crisis, like a re-structure, news of an impending re-structure, or after a number of senior dismissals or retrenchments. In meetings where this UGR is prominent, the objective is not to speak – or if required to speak, to say as little as possible.

At our management meetings, the aim is to impress the boss

When this UGR is in force, meetings are competition for air space. Managers seek to ensure that all others are aware of their significance. Their strategy might be via highlighting outcomes/achievements, or it might be via the 'smart talk trap', mentioned earlier.

Among the trusted group, it's OK to joke about the incompetence of some of our manager colleagues

This UGR requires a group of managers to form sufficient trust for them to comment on inadequacies of one or more of their colleagues. Prior to this trust being established, one or more of the group will push the barriers of accepted discussion content. At first, the comment might be a short quip or even a facial expression. If the remark or comment is accepted, another of the group might build on this in a small way. These 'trust games' are played until the discussion territory includes the opportunity to comment on the failings or weaknesses of other managers. The level of trust within management cliques is rapidly speeded up if there are opportunities to network in a social context. The informal nature of a social drinks along with the inhibitions fostered after suitable amounts of alcohol combine to promote and build this UGR.

The boss plays 'ducks and drakes' with us to ensure we are kept out of the picture, and to build his kudos with his manager

This UGR emerges when a group or sub-group of managers believe the boss is not being completely open and honest. When this emerges, these managers look deeply into the meaning behind the boss' messages, comments and strategies, to determine the real agenda. This sometimes results in managers agreeing on and being driven by a 'secret agenda' that has never been espoused by the boss. This inferred 'secret agenda' can also be wrong!

We build our credibility by referring to our recent conversations with the CEO, or executives from other organizations

This UGR surfaces where managers feel insecure for whatever reasons. These managers seek to reinforce and build their credibility in the eyes of other managers and in the eyes of their staff by name-dropping. They will say for example, 'When I was talking with the CEO yesterday, he said...' Alternatively, the comment might be 'That's not on the CEO's agenda based on the discussion I had last night. She said...'

These managers may also refer to discussions with well-known executives from other businesses.

The next set of sample UGRs relates to *Management UGRs about staff*.

Staff cannot be trusted – if they get the chance to use our corporate intelligence they will set up their own business and use it

Over the last decade, changes to the structure and size of corporations have resulted in the emergence of a large number of small consulting businesses, often comprising only one person who has left a larger organization. It has not been uncommon for these people to subsequently be contracted into the organization from which they departed, at rates much higher than they were paid as full time staff. Indeed, some individuals have set up their own businesses as direct competitors to their previous employer. This has resulted in levels of distrust such as this UGR, which is applied to all staff.

There are only a few staff who are truly committed – most of them are here for the pay cheque

This self-perpetuating UGR is prominent in many organizations. If staff are thought not to be committed, they will be treated as such. If they are treated poorly, they will not be committed.

We avoid dealing with really difficult staff by offloading poor performers onto other managers wherever possible

Time and again I have seen managers fail to directly address the issue of a poor performer. On many occasions the 'strategy' to deal with the troublesome person or poor performer is to wait for the opportunity, then organise an internal transfer into another department or another location.

We act as consultative, because the CEO says it's important, but behind closed doors we use creative means to push our own agenda

This UGR is prominent in organizations where there is a lack of alignment between what people say and what they do. The 'talk' espoused by the CEO in these organizations is parroted by the next line of managers because 'this is the way we talk about ourselves'. These senior managers may well be intelligent, well qualified people and in some instances they may be unaware that what they say does not correspond with what they do. In more sinister cases however, this UGR is prominent where managers are playing for political points in front of the CEO and other managers, while at the same time having no intention of carrying out what they espouse.

If we want something done, we confide with a few select staff who are willing to back us, and who are willing to act on our behalf

This UGR can occur unwittingly or by design. It occurs unwittingly in cases where managers identify with staff who are seen to support their views. It follows that these managers will then use these staff as sounding boards, and in some cases as change agents to help effect changes that the managers want implemented. Again, this UGR can arise by design in circumstances where managers single out those staff who are most useful for them given the nature of the required change and the current circumstances of the work team. These staff are then 'used' as change agents. Interestingly, whether unwittingly or by design, this UGR gives rise to another UGR perceived by staff which is 'around here, staff are 'used' by managers – once they have done what managers want, they are left high and dry'.

We build our importance by referring to staff as 'my staff'

On many occasions I have heard managers referring to their people as 'my staff', or 'my people'. This UGR helps to reinforce the manager's importance, but it does little for that manager's subordinates, as to many it carries with it a patronising tone.

Different UGRs in Different Organizational Types

Deal and Kennedy (2000) describe four broad types of organizations that demonstrate very different cultures. They first identify two dimensions on which to differentiate organizations:

- The degree of risk associated with a company's key activities. In some environments, the stakes are high. In others the risks are fairly minimal.
- The speed at which a company and its staff get feedback on whether decisions or strategies are successful.

Using these two dimensions enables us to generate quadrants as is shown below in Figure 1. The 'All or Nothing' organization includes management consulting, investment banking and advertising companies. The 'Work Hard/Play Hard' quadrant refers to the likes of computer companies, high technology start ups, and auto retailing. The 'Bet Your Company' organizations include mining and smelting companies, oil companies and architectural firms. The 'Process' quadrant refers to banks, government agencies and regulated industries.

Not surprisingly, the UGRs in each of these quadrants differ quite dramatically from one another. This is an important point which is worthy of being emphasised – there is no 'universal set' of UGRs that are 'right' for all organizations. Apart from those UGRs that pertain to how people treat each other within an organization, the optimum set of UGRs in any company will depend on their industry and organizational contexts. Management consulting and investment banking companies (i.e. 'All or Nothing' organizations) will have UGRs that are very different from government agencies and regulated industries (i.e. 'Process' organizations). Similarly, the UGRs in mining and smelting companies (i.e. 'Bet Your Company' organizations) will differ substantially from those in computer and auto retailing companies (i.e. 'Work Hard/Play Hard' organizations).

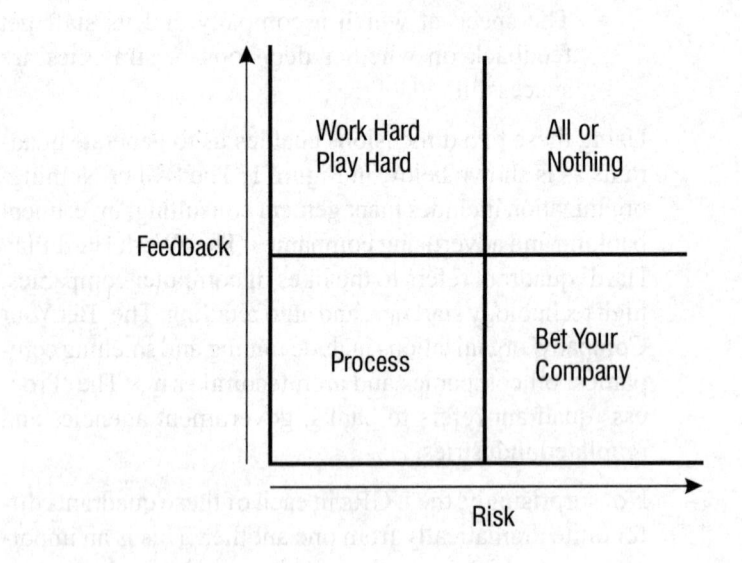

Figure 1:
Organizational 'type' matrix

Feedback ↑	Work Hard Play Hard	All or Nothing
	Process	Bet Your Company

Risk →

UGRs and Value Statements

When people are first introduced to UGRs, it is not uncommon for some to ask about the relationship between UGRs and value statements. This is an interesting issue as, on the surface, they are difficult to differentiate.

Value statements represent what is thought to be the 'common beliefs' about what is most important to a team or organization. They are normally derived from strategic or business planning sessions where management and/or staff thrash out what the group ought to believe as important. These are agreed on, recorded and form part of the business planning documentation. They represent the outcomes from one or more meetings.

UGRs are people's perception of common beliefs, inferred from actions that happen, or fail to happen. In a sense, UGRs are 'inferred values', as they are derived from the conclusions people make from behaviours.

I once worked with an organization soon after it had gone through a fairly extensive strategic planning process. Of course, part of that process involved the generation of a number of value statements. Upon introducing the management to the concept of UGRs, there was a degree of alarm and confusion about the 'true value' of their recently framed value statements!

In what proved to be a very interesting exercise, they subsequently explored the possible UGRs that might work against their value statements. Extracts from this are reported in the table that follows.

Value Statement	UGRs that Would Work Against the Value.
	Around here…
Trust - Our organization is open and accountable	• We keep things close to our chest, and only reveal information on a 'need to know' basis
	• When you ask someone to keep something 'in confidence', you can guarantee everyone will find out about it
	• We long for the days when we could just do what we wanted to do
	• The only way we are kept up to date is when we ask the 'right' people the 'right' questions
	• We think of creative ways to present the 'real' truth
Respect - We treat each other with respect at all times. We are courteous and value other opinions	• At staff meetings, people's eyes are always pointing down
	• Different points of view are a pain in the neck
	• People over-talk others when they speak for too long, or when their opinion carries no weight
	• When some bosses attend meetings, people filter what they would otherwise say
	• People are treated differently when the senior bosses are around

Teamwork - We work together to achieve positive outcomes and respect the collaborative democratic decision making process

- In meetings where there are different levels of staff, the 'junior' staff are never asked to contribute their point of view
- What the boss says 'goes'
- People who have a different point of view from the mainstream are made to feel isolated
- At meetings where there are differences in views, eyes begin to roll
- Teamwork is talked about, but the work always rests on the shoulders of the typical one or two people
- You can't rely on jobs being done – if you want something done you're better off doing it yourself
- Some people's opinions carry no weight

Responsiveness - We respond to issues promptly and encourage customer involvement

- The organization talks about customer involvement, but essentially it is a pain and we're better off not having it
- The speed with which we respond to issues depends on who is complaining
- If possible, we pass on jobs to someone else
- When we say that we will do something, there is a 50-50 chance it will happen

Service - We exist to serve our customers and seek to continually improve all that we do

- Service is a job for front line staff, and if only they would show a little more initiative

- Continuous improvement is unrealistic in our work – our goal is to keep the lid on problems

- Being customer focussed is an invitation for more complaints, which we can do without

- People are punished for giving good service – as they get a reputation for being 'good', and more work is referred to them

Best Practice - We conduct ourselves professionally at all times. We encourage innovation and develop/ resource all our people to achieve the organization's mission

- 'Best Practice' is considered just another buzz word, which will pass with time

- We only need to be 'professional' when the senior bosses or whistleblowers are around

- There is talk about developing/ resourcing people, but when it comes to the crunch there is never a budget for it

- Innovation is OK, as long as it doesn't involve extra dollars, and it doesn't impact on other departments

This proved to be an insightful and useful way to think about the relationship between UGRs and Values Statements. Indeed, it would seem to be an important consideration for any team or corporation going through the strategic planning process. But more on that later…

In a Nutshell

- The simplest way to think about organizational culture is 'this is the way we do things around here'. Unwritten Ground Rules (UGRs) are people's perceptions of 'the way we do things around here', and they are inferred from the behaviours of others in the organization. Incredibly, UGRs are rarely talked about

- UGRs are a potent force that dictate how people behave. Sometimes, UGRs exist and yet no-one is able to explain why. If you ever doubt this, think of the story of the five monkeys!

- A core set of UGRs is mutually reinforced within a team. These UGRs define the behaviour of a team, and there are strong negative consequences if they are defied. Central to the core set of UGRs is the issue of trust – and whether or not a team member can be trusted to act in accordance with the team's UGRs. To defy UGRs is a major breach of trust that brings major consequences, not least being alienation from the team

- UGRs that exist in some companies include, 'Around here':
  - Keep quiet in meetings and you do not get extra jobs
  - An individual's standing is related to how they relate in a social context with senior management
  - Part time staff are not 'real' staff
  - Opposing views are a personal attack

- Being open and honest scars you for life, particularly if it relates in a negative way towards senior management
- Because UGRs are people's perceptions of 'the way we do things around here', there will always be varying levels of agreement on UGRs. 'Strong' cultures will have higher levels of UGR agreement than 'weak' cultures
- UGRs exist for managers as well as staff. Management UGRs in some companies include, 'Around here':
  - At our management meetings, the aim is to impress the boss
  - The boss plays 'Ducks and Drakes' with us to ensure we are kept out of the picture, and to build his kudos with his manager
  - There are only a few staff who are truly committed – most of them are here for the pay cheque
  - We act as consultative, because the CEO says it's important, but behind closed doors we use creative means to push our own agenda
  - We build our importance by referring to staff as 'my staff'
- The 'optimum' UGRs in any company will depend on the organization type – and whether or not there are high levels of risk in its operations, and whether or not there are high levels of feedback
- Value Statements are normally framed during business planning sessions involving senior management. Sometimes, the outcomes from these sessions are disseminated to staff across the organization. UGRs are people's perception of

common beliefs, inferred from actions that happen or fail to happen. In a sense, UGRs are 'inferred values'

UGRs in a Different Context

> Leadership is action, not position.
> Donald H Mcgannon

At this point, it is important that we remind ourselves that not all UGRs are negative. There are many work teams and organizations that are prospering from a positive team culture that is underpinned by positive UGRs. In my view, these teams and organizations are in the minority, and they are currently earning a reputation for outstanding service – a reputation that is all too scarce nowadays.

My point in painting the picture so far is to highlight the fact that it does not matter what service strategies or tactics we deploy if the UGRs are negative. UGRs will win every time.

I have found it fascinating to consider the notion of UGRs in teams outside of a work situation. As I have been involved with, and continue to have an interest in a wide range of sports, I have found genuine value in exploring UGRs in this context.

In just about any team sport you like to consider, there are some common behaviours that occur among members of the same team. I think these demonstrate some UGRs that are firmly in place, and that are well worth considering.

A Goal is Scored

In all team sports, when a person scores or shoots a goal, there is normally a celebration (to varying degrees, depending on the sport!). Often, the person who has scored the goal will then do something that is significant – they will point up the ground or pitch, and yell out something to a teammate. Sometimes, these players will physically run up the ground or pitch to another team member, and pat them on the back.

This happens in soccer, basketball, rugby, hockey and every other team sport of which I am aware.

What the goal scorer is doing is giving recognition to the person who gave them the opportunity to shoot the goal. They are recognizing the hard work that went into getting the ball to them (as a shooter/scorer).

The very strong UGR in sporting teams is this:

Around here, we always recognise the hard work done by our team mates before us

This recognition is not confined to the full forwards. The full forwards will thank the half forwards, the half forwards will thank the centres, the centres will thank the half backs, and the half backs will thank the backs. Sometimes the recognition is not obvious to spectators but in good teams it always happens.

Teams practice this at training and do it in the game. Week in, week out, they practice recognition and do it in the game. There is no policy document that stipulates that this must be done, but it happens, game after game, year after year.

How Important is the Individual?

During 1999, there was an incredible record broken by an individual in a team sport. This record had stood for 62 years – a remarkable length of time, and one that probably is as long standing a record as just about any major sport across the world.

The record was in Australian Rules Football. Tony Lockett, a full forward broke the record for career goals, a record that had stood for 62 years.

Immediately after the game, a television reporter interviewed Lockett. The interview began something like this:

> 'Plugger (Lockett's nickname), do you realise the magnitude of the record you have just broken today'
>
> 'Probably not, to be honest, I'm just happy we won'

This is an amazing response when you stop and think about it. Here is a man who has broken a record that has stood for 62 years, and he is saying 'I'm just happy we won'.

This is a powerful UGR that is prominent in all team sports. It is:

Around here, team is more important than the individual

There is ample evidence that this UGR is an integral part of sport. Recently, Bob Skilton, an ex Australian Rules Footballer was interviewed on the radio. Skilton was a champion player. He had won three Brownlow Medals, the highest accolade for an individual in the sport. No one has won more than three Brownlow Medals. Skilton said 'I would gladly trade my three Brownlow Medals for a grand final win'.

Skilton played in teams that never won a grand final. Once again, Skilton was reinforcing a powerful UGR in sporting teams – 'Team is more important than the individual'. No one was prompting Skilton – no one was telling him to read a policy – he said what he felt and he meant what he said.

In 1998, Mark Taylor, the then captain of the Australian Cricket team, had a marvellous period with the bat when playing against Pakistan at Peshawar. At the end of the third day's play, Taylor was on 334 not out, equal with the all time record score for an Australian in test matches, set by the great Sir Donald Bradman against England in 1930.

Taylor declared at the overnight score.

In the interests of giving the team a chance to win that game (as it turned out the game was drawn), Taylor sacrificed his individual achievement for the team. He could have batted for five minutes the following day and broken the record set by Bradman, and then declared. But in the interest of the team, he did not. Further reinforcement of this powerful UGR – 'Team is more important than the individual'.

Time for Performance Review

Recently I discovered something about Australian Rules Football that I had previously not been aware of. I discovered that every player is video taped for the entire game, every week. In the week following the game, each player sits with their specialist coach and they watch the video. The specialist coach will talk through the video with the player – pointing out what was done well, what was done poorly and exploring options.

This is done with every player, every week. The captain of the team engages in it, as does the player who is battling to make the team.

The UGR here is as follows:

Around here, individual performance in analysed with a view to improvement, without it being a personal attack

It could be argued that these selected UGRs in selected sporting circumstances lose credibility in their application to a business context because of the very fact that they are selective. Interestingly, there is evidence of a wide range of positively oriented UGRs in the organizations that support 'Peak Performance' sporting teams.

In their recently published book 'Peak Performance[18]', authors Gilson, Pratt, Roberts and Weyms, profile characteristics of the organizations that are behind world-elite professional sporting teams – the teams with outstanding and long-term achievements that are unlikely to be matched in the near future. In the following segment, we draw key points from three Peak Performance organizations profiled in that book to highlight the UGRs that underpin their success.

The Australian Women's Field Hockey Team

Since 1988, the Australian Women's Field Hockey team has won three Olympic gold medals – in 1988, 1996 and 2000, the 1998 Commonwealth Games gold medal, two gold medals at the World Championships in 1994 and 1998 and gold medals for the last five Champions Trophy tournaments since 1991. It has an 80% win record in over 200 international games over the last decade.

The Office/Administrative Environment

In profiling the office and administrative environment of Women's Hockey Australia (WHA), authors Gilson et al make particular reference to:

- A strong sense of shared purpose
- A tempo and feel of the administration that is high, but not frenetic.
- A calm, coordinated activity with no obvious locus of control which creates an impression of flow

Given these observations, what would be the prevailing UGRs? I think they may be as follows:

- Around here, we feel we are all here working towards the same goal
- Around here, we're busy, but we never let that lapse into panic!
- Around here, we're all responsible people whose focus is on getting the job done, not who has power over whom

Management Orientation

The management orientation of WHA is characterised as follows:

- There is an ambience of friendly informality
- Each committee is held accountable to measurable objectives
- The President spends time in the office helping to establish informality, heaping plenty of praise on deserving staff and demonstrating passion and interest in the tasks undertaken
- The General Manager holds informal weekly management meetings to ensure the organization is 'happy and harmonious'
- The organization is a very self critical organization (more so than any of the other nine world renowned organizations profiled in the book)
- Board members rarely express satisfaction with current performance
- The push to exceed personal best is relentless

A member of the Board of Directors talks about the WHA environment as follows:

> '(Within WHA there is a) respect for each other, love of the game, plus a determination to succeed. It's not much different from being a player. In an organization such as this, either on the Board or in the National Office, you still attack the job in the same manner, you set yourself goals just as you did as a player. It makes no difference if we are talking strategic plans, budgets or whatever, you still have to see the bigger picture, which is what we had to do when we were playing. If we could have our time over again we would still rather be out on a paddock than in the boardroom or office. Our collective memory keeps it together.'[19]

Given these observations, what are the UGRs? I think they might include the following:

- Around here, there's no need for 'airs and graces', as we're all important - so we sustain a positive, friendly work environment
- Around here, individual and team performance is taken seriously, with a view to improvement, so we're happy to be held accountable
- Around here, the boss cares passionately about our performance, and really appreciates people's good performance
- Around here, the General Manager ensures we're all fully informed
- Around here, good enough is never good enough - while we appreciate good performance, we know we can always do better

Coaching/Playing Orientation

Then coach, Rick Charlesworth was described as a unique man, who is 'probably the best coach in the world'[20]. A past player described Charlesworth as follows:

> '..Coach Rick Charlesworth demands so much of himself and you know he will demand the same of you. He's just got that competitiveness which is fantastic. You would lie down and die for him if that enabled someone to score a goal for us'[21]

Coach Charlesworth gives an insight into his coaching philosophy:

> 'Everybody gets carried away with the score. I like to develop different attitudes in players. One of the most critical things

that you have to do is develop an attitude which is analytical and clinical. We keep a lot of statistics to help us look closely at everything that happens. Each person gets an efficiency rating for every game they play, so we know that if they get the ball 45 times and they turned it over 45 times, that is not good – or if they turned it over twice and they were penetrating on 15 occasions then that's very good and their efficiency rating is 95% or whatever. This enables players to look behind the results. They can be honest in a way that is not threatening. It's all about improving. If you improve yourself, you will beat the opposition. We actually don't go out there to win, we go out to play well and winning is the by-product of that. The focus is on how we play rather than the outcome.'[22]

Charlesworth deployed a 'No bench' policy – every player was in the team and expected to play. With a 'bench' the implicit message is that these players are not good enough, which is a message they begin to believe. The players all expected to be rotated on and off the bench during a game – including the most skilled and valued players.

Interpreting the UGRs from coach Charlesworth is of particular interest. Here is a list of those I think are prominent:

- Around here, the boss is fiercely competitive, but will not ask you to do anything he wouldn't do himself
- Around here, the boss does what he says he will do
- Around here our performance is analysed and measured as a tool to help us improve
- Around here, the driving force is individual and team improvement. Outcomes are the consequence of improvement, outcomes are not our first priority

- Around here, every person in the team is valuable and plays their part. No one is more important than anyone else

The Chicago Bulls Basketball Team

In 1998 the Chicago Bulls won its sixth National Basketball Championship. This was their 14th straight NBA Championship playoff appearance. From 1990 the team won six championship rings in eight years. The loss in 1999 of super-star Michael Jordon, along with Coach Jackson, as well as Dennis Rodman, Luc Longley and Scottie Pippen saw the team fall from first to last. In their analysis of World 'Peak Performance' teams, Gilson et al (2000) believe it will not be long before the Chicago Bulls are back at the top of the field.

The Office/Administrative Environment

Gilson et al (2000) make some fascinating observations about the office and administrative aspects of the Chicago Bulls that include:

- On the office walls hang action-laden photographs, mounted press clippings, signed basketballs and singlets celebrating the Bulls' history. The office floor is wooden boards with court markings
- Inside the office, 'smiles come easily', reflecting a close knit community that is fun-loving, respectful and professional

It could be inferred from these simple observations that the following UGRs are in place:

- Around here, our history is important, and we're proud of it
- Around here, our premises are structured to constantly remind us of the 'bigger picture'
- Around here, we are more a community than a team – we care, we have fun, and we respect one another

Management Orientation

The Chicago Bulls have very strong principles that guide the management team. The organization is made up of seven departments, responsible for 32 front office staff and around 20 assistant coaches, trainers, medical staff and media announcers. Including the on-court players, the entire organization comprises less than 70 people. According to Gilson et al, in an organization that is not built with multiple layers, owner and Chairman, Jerry Reinsdorf gives his three vice presidents a great deal of leeway, independence, responsibility and jurisdiction. Vice President, Irwin Mandel reports on the opportunity to go to Chairman Reinsdorf directly without having first to go to a president, or vice chairman. Reinsdorf 'is a decisive person' who allows people to make their case directly and quickly.

The Director of Sales at the Chicago Bulls said:

> 'If there is something that I think will make my department or any area of the Bulls more efficient, I can go to my vice president and we can debate the pros and cons, and if we like the idea the decision is made right there, it's done. Even if it's a decision that involves a substantial investment. If we like an idea, we can pick up the phone and call our owner, Jerry Reinsdorf, who is extremely accessible, and Jerry will give you a 'Yes, go ahead it's a great idea', or 'No, it's not', and things get done very quickly and very easily. There isn't a lot

of red tape or paperwork. Our management structure is well defined and pretty streamlined.'[23]

Although in short supply (people employed by the Chicago Bulls tend to remain a very long time), when filling vacancies for positions in the company, the valued criteria are good people of good character, and people who are happy and are fun to be with. The philosophy has been to promote from within. If there are no career possibilities within the business, there is great pride taken from seeing people go to 'bigger and better' things outside the organization.

Senior Director of Media Services, Tim Hallem, commented on the tone of the office:

> 'People are friendly. Probably 90% of the people in this building are here because they enjoy sports of some form or another and wanted to get into sports marketing and public relations.
>
> ...I walk into work each day. It's friendly, it's informal, yet respectful. You're genuinely curious about their life, their family, their children, as well as what's going on with the Bulls. I've been here long enough to see Irwin's kids go from three years old to college. We've seen people struggle through deaths, personal problems, divorces and at the same time we've all laughed ourselves silly. We've enjoyed ourselves and we've frequently worked ourselves to exhaustion'[24]

Gilson et al make these other points about the Bulls:

- There is an ambience of informality. Even on game day, there is an absence of meetings. Instead, people talk all the time, sharing information
- Everyone in the organization is expected to contribute in an active or passive way to a successful sale of season tickets. Ideas are constantly provided to ensure that, whatever the result of the game, the

entertainment package is the best that it can be. Staff visit Disney and NBA marketing meetings to assist their creativity

'We have four full-time service representatives whose sole job is to meet face to face each year with every single Bulls season ticket holder. They actually go to their place of business or home, knock on the door, walk in and say hello. They let them know that we appreciate their support for the Bulls... We always hand over a small gift to them at this time.'[25]

- The organization look to engage sponsors who will be committed to the Bulls for longer than the run of success enjoyed while Michael Jordon was playing. They hoped to have established strong relationships that provide benefits irrespective of the on court success

Based on these comments and observations, I would presume the following UGRs would be in place with regard to the management orientation at the Chicago Bulls:

- Around here, management has the authority and will to make decisions, and they are approachable if you have an idea or question in mind

- Around here, management does not get hung up about which staff talk to which managers

- Around here, we care about one another – we promote from within, select new staff on their propensity to be good team players, and we take pride in our people moving on to bigger and better things

- Around here, we truly work as a team – we pay attention to people's personal lives, we pitch in together, and we have fun
- Around here, while we have our own jobs, we are all aware of the bigger picture, and the need to sell season tickets, so we all pitch in, in whatever way we can
- Around here, our customers and our sponsors are our lifeline, so we make every effort to ensure they get value from their relationship with us

The New Zealand Rugby Union Football Team

The New Zealand All Blacks Rugby Union team has a win ration of over 72%. In a country with a population of just over 3.8 million, the team has a wonderful record in rugby union, being placed in the top three in each of the 1987, 1991 and 1995 rugby World Cups, and winning in 1987. Although their performance was disappointing in the 1999 World Cup, their record over the past 100 years has been outstanding.

The Office/Administrative Environment

Gilson et al make the point that the All Blacks office and administrative environment is one that reflects real alignment with the All Black playing philosophy.

As with players, the driving force behind administrative staff in the national office is personal responsibility and an overwhelming passion to improve and 'do better'

'We want people in here who are going to be self starters, motivated and actually go off and do it. People here understand that we are not going to be just reactive. I encourage that. I don't want to run this business, I want my people to run it. We foster a culture of hard work, commitment and passion. Passion for everything we do, but specifically passion for the All Blacks. There are no half measures. If you're not passionate about the All Blacks, don't come and work here.'[26]

From these observations, I would propose the following UGRs being in place:

- Around here, we take personal responsibility for our own jobs, and there is a common drive to constantly seek to do better
- Around here, near enough is not good enough
- Around here, we truly believe in the value of our work and our cause

Management Orientation

With regard to the management team of the All Blacks, Gilson et al make the following points:

- There is a very strong sense of 'Once an All Black, always an All Black' – the New Zealand Rugby Football Union (NZRFU) has made astute appointments to ensure that the organization never loses its memory and experience of being an All Black. The sense of community that has been built across generations has been sustained by appointing past All Black players to key positions
- There is a constant updating of strategic documents, with mid year summits and the like. The 1998 annual report details six key measures of success that are addressed by 25 strategic objectives against which progress is matched

'(CEO David Moffett) has the ability to get down to what needs to be done, rather than get lost in the woods. He has terrific vision of where this game needs to go, and is a true agent of change. You can't underestimate what he's done in pulling the whole group together, and in identifying the right organizational players. That's the story here, David's ability to attract the right people.'[27]

'Everybody has input, everybody is listened to, everybody is a valuable unit in here. It's the little things that count, like the Monday morning work in progress meetings where we all find out what's happening and where we are at, so that we are all absolutely accountable for what we do. This makes our teams very fluid. We know each others' jobs pretty well, so that we take responsibility for the total result, not just our component of it. We love breaking down walls.'[28]

From these small insights, I think the UGRs with regard to management of the All Blacks might be as follows:

- Around here, we are proud of our history, and seek to find ways in which this history is constantly told and reinforced

- Around here, our plans are real – we work to them, we are measured by them, and we regularly review them

- Around here, management has a very clear vision, and we're all headed in that direction

- Around here, everyone knows their job, everyone is genuinely listened to, irrespective of their level, and we're all prepared to pitch in and help one another

These sample UGRs in sporting organizations raise some interesting questions. We have a collection of people in this activity called 'work' and we often have UGRs that are negative and destructive.

We have another collection of people in this activity called 'sport' and we have positive UGRs. Why is there a difference?

I have had some interesting responses to this question when I have posed it during presentations. Some of the responses I have received include:

- In sporting teams they have a visible goal (the scoreboard) and the game is only for a short term (although my response to this is that UGRs exist in professional teams where the sport is their work)
- At work, we tend not to have goals, we just come along day after day
- People like playing sport....

This latter response is one that I find intriguing. Of course the implication is that people generally do not like work, but this can be taken to another level. We all know people who play in the lowest grade competition of sport, their team gets beaten week in, week out and these people are still battling to make the team. **Maybe the reason people like playing team sports is because of the UGRs!**

While it is interesting to consider, I do not like to focus too long on a comparison between sport and work. I do not think that gets us anywhere, and there are more important questions which are:

- How are UGRs established?
- Are we able to import some of the positive UGRs in sport into our workplace?

In a Nutshell

- UGRs are not all negatively oriented! Team sports are often characterised by their positively focussed UGRs that include 'Around here, we always recognise the teamwork done by our team mates before us', 'Around here team is more important than the individual', 'Around here, individual performance is analysed with a view to improvement, without it being a personal attack'
- In 'Peak Performance' teams – sporting organizations that have reached and stayed at the top of their sport, the organizations that sit behind the players often are characterised by positive UGRs. These are the businesses behind the sporting teams which appear to have UGRs that include the following:
    - Around here, we feel we are all here working towards the same goal
    - Around here, we're busy, but we never let that lapse into panic!
    - Around here, there's no need for 'airs and graces', as we're all important - so we sustain a positive, friendly work environment

- Around here, individual and team performance is taken seriously, with a view to improvement, so we're happy to be held accountable
- Around here, the boss cares passionately about our performance, and really appreciates people's good performance
- Around here, good enough is never good enough - while we appreciate good performance, we know we can always do better
- Around here, the boss is fiercely competitive, but will not ask you to do anything he wouldn't do himself
- Around here, the boss does what he says he will do
- Around here, the driving force is individual and team improvement. Outcomes are the consequence of improvement, outcomes are not our first priority
- Around here, every person in the team is valuable and plays their part. No one is more important than anyone else
- Around here, our history is important, and we're proud of it
- Around here, our premises are structured to constantly remind us of the 'bigger picture'
- Around here, management have the authority and will to make decisions, and they are approachable if you have an idea or question in mind
- Around here, management don't get hung up about which staff talk to which managers

- Around here, we care about one another – we promote from within, select new staff on their propensity to be good team players, and we take pride in our people moving on to bigger and better things
- Around here, we truly work as a team – we pay attention to people's personal lives, we pitch in together, and we have fun
- Around here, while we have our own jobs, we are all aware of the bigger picture, and the need to sell season tickets, so we all pitch in, in whatever way we can
- Around here, our customers and our sponsors are our lifeline, so we make every effort to ensure they get value from their relationships with us

How are UGRs established?

UGRs exist in every organization - so they are set somehow!

Let me address how UGRs are established by diverting for a moment to another view I have about people in organizations.

People can be classified as belonging to one of two broad groups (probably most of us are somewhere in between these two groups, but bear with me!). These two groups are represented in the diagram below:

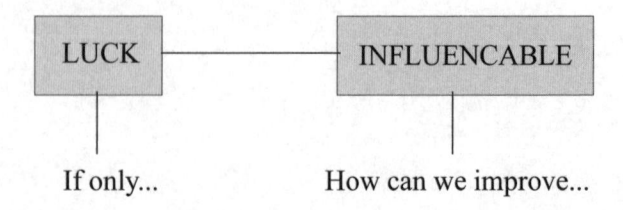

```
    ┌─────────┐              ┌──────────────┐
    │  LUCK   │──────────────│ INFLUENCABLE │
    └─────────┘              └──────────────┘
         │                          │
     If only...              How can we improve...
```

The **'LUCK'** people in an organization are heard to say:
- If only she wasn't in our branch
- If only we had a different boss
- If only we could do this...

This kind of thinking says that it doesn't matter what we do, things will always be the same

The **'INFLUENCABLE'** people in a business can be heard to say:
- We've got a problem here, how do *you* think we can get over it
- I need help to do this - *I'm* having problems at the moment
- Can I tell you how I feel about this issue...?

This kind of thinking says we can and **will** work better together!

'Luck' people are victims. Things are the way they are because of luck - usually bad luck. Things will only change if they are lucky - or unlucky. These people have an external locus of control.

'Influencable' people believe that most things are able to be influenced. They are masters of their own destiny. They believe, genuinely, that we are able to change things if we want things to change. **They believe we can set UGRs, and have a desire to make and keep them positive**.

UGRs represent 'the way we do things around here'. UGRs are deduced, and in the past have rarely, if ever, been made explicit. If the spoken or written word has clashed with UGRs, then the UGRs will win every time.

UGRs have been established as part of the history of the organization. They are set by senior people – and staff perception of the *alignment* between what these senior people say and what they do.

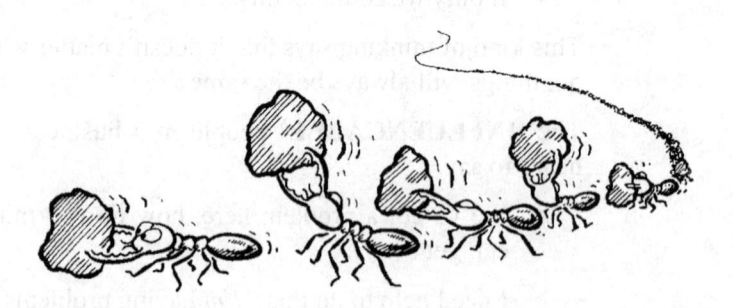

The management of an organization may allude for example, to the value and importance of customer service. They may raise the issue time and again at staff meetings, with proclamations that 'the customer is always right', and 'nobody ever wins an argument with a customer'.

If the management fail to do what they say, then they are automatically setting some UGRs.

As an example, consider a scenario where the General Manager of an organization mouths some customer service platitudes at a staff meeting. The next day a very unhappy customer comes into the premises - this person is obviously angry and upset, demanding to speak to the General Manager.

The General Manager listens to the customer for a short time and then starts to deny any responsibility for the customer's problem. An argument ensues and the shouting match can be heard across a large area of the premises. The customer leaves, more angry and upset than when they entered, with threats of legal action to follow.

The UGRs here are:

- Around here, if the customer complains about our services, then there is a fair chance they are dishonest, and they are trying to take advantage of us
- Around here it is OK to yell and shout at a customer if we think they are in the wrong, and if the customer is bad enough

Importantly, if the majority of people in this organization are 'Luck' people, then these negative UGRs will become entrenched in the organization. The platitudes may continue to be mouthed, but people will know that this is not *really* the way things are around here. Remember, 'Luck' people think that things are the way they are because of luck, so these people would wait until someone else changed things around here. While this manager remained, it is unlikely anything would change, so the UGRs would lock in even stronger.

An interesting development would occur however, if the General Manager criticized a staff member for displaying the same behaviour in yelling at a customer. In this case, some other UGRs would emerge:

- Around here, there are two sets of rules – one for the General Manager, and one for us
- Around here, it's OK to yell at customers as long as the boss never hears you doing this

These UGRs would have tremendous power and would be passed on from staff to staff.

If on the other hand, the majority of staff at this organization were 'Influencable' people, then they could confront the management to share their views. This is a critical point in the evolution of UGRs, as the General Manager's response would set in place behaviour to follow.

If, on hearing the staff members' concern, the General Manager agreed with them and thanked them for highlighting the problem, some interesting UGRs would surface:

- Around here, it's OK to share your concerns with the boss
- Around here, the boss will listen to any suggestions you might have for improvement
- Around here, customer service is a real priority, and if that means hauling the boss over the coals, so be it

If on the other hand the General Manager got upset at this viewpoint being put to him/her, some other UGRs would emerge:

- Around here, being honest doesn't pay
- Around here, you can't trust the boss who says one thing but means another
- Around here, the only reason we should focus on service is because the boss wants us to

UGRs build up over time, and the longer they are in place, the more difficult they are to change. They are extremely unlikely to change while the majority of people in a team or organization are 'Luck' people.

One final word of caution here: 'Influencable' people are not always positively oriented. In some cases, people manipulate the culture so that it is negatively oriented, and they perceive that it is in their interest to sustain the negative UGRs.

In some cases, UGRs are manipulated as a defence mechanism by managers who feel inadequate about aspects of their personal performance at work. These people feel that if they were exposed for their real knowledge or skills, that would be used against them and they would lose their power or influence over people (interestingly, another UGR!). In this context, UGRs are used as a defence mechanism to protect a personally perceived inadequacy. As an example, a manager may feel inadequate about his/her personal skills to deal with an angry customer. This manager might proclaim the importance of service on a regular basis, but when it comes to assisting a staff member to deal with a difficult customer, this manager might become aloof, or might say to the staff member 'You've got to learn to deal with these people – I can't be around to help you all the time.'

In other cases, UGRs are created by staff or managers who are in a competitive context and where they wish to obtain an advantage over their peers. They wish to be seen in a better light by more senior colleagues and attempt to gain political advantage over their 'competitors' who might be in different departments or different geographical locations. As an example, a manager might be seen to proclaim the importance of customer service on a regular basis. This manager however, might abandon his/her involvement in an important staff meeting dedicated to service, if there was a chance for that manager to meet personally with a senior manager. This would be an example of 'political manoeuvring' being more important than customer service, and negative UGRs would follow.

A key question with regard to UGRs is whether or not they can be changed...

In a Nutshell

- In essence, we can classify people into one of two groups – 'Luck' people believe that the way things are is because of luck – normally 'bad' luck. 'Luck' people wait for good luck, and normally they have to wait for a very long time. 'Influencable' people believe that they are able to influence most things. If they see something they do not like or agree with, they first determine whether other people see things the same way, and then they say, 'Well what are we going to do about it?' With knowledge about UGRs, 'Influencable' people seek to make changes to those UGRs they think could be improved

- UGRs have been established as part of the history of a team or organization. They are people's perceptions of the alignment between what others say and what they do – in particular the senior management. If management fail to do what they say, negative UGRs will then be created or reinforced

- Some people deliberately manipulate UGRs as a defence mechanism to cover for their own sense of inadequacy

- Some people create UGRs when they display behaviour that is intended to help them gain a competitive advantage over others

- Other people create UGRs without even knowing it!

- The key question from all this is 'Can UGRs be changed?'

Can UGRs Be Changed?

> In an earthquake, the most dangerous place to be is in a tall building that is not flexible. Yet, one of the safest places is a tall building that has been stressed for earthquakes - in other words, one that has a deep foundation and is flexible. So, too, over the coming years, large organizations that remain rigid will crumble and fall, while those that succeed in adding flexibility, teamwork and creativity to their cultures will thrive. – Source unknown

UGRs are the foundation of service in any organization. They dictate how people behave towards each other, and they dictate the level of service that is provided both to external and internal customers.

Given that they are so powerful, the key question is whether or not they can be changed, and if so how?

In my view, there are *direct* and *indirect* ways in which organizations and teams can work to change UGRs. The indirect methods, which in one sense should not be undervalued, are the range of strategies and tactics, examples of which were given at the beginning of this book.

Indirect Cultural Change Methods

Most organizations attempt to develop a culture of service via indirect methods. These organizations may mention the term 'culture', but the strategies and tactics do not address the culture directly. In these cases, the organization adopts 'special initiatives' that for example are more customer focussed, in the belief that the culture will similarly improve.

Indirect strategies work in organizations where coincidentally, there is *alignment* between what people say they do, and what people actually do. In these cases, the philosophies and values that underpin the change tactics and strategies are consistent with the behaviours that management and staff display. The UGRs are positive, but are not articulated.

These organizations can be very efficient, profitable and team oriented workplaces. I have come across only a few of these organizations, as they are in the minority.

Many organizations that I have encountered are trying to keep up with the competition by deploying various change-oriented initiatives, while at the same time sustaining at least some UGRs that are sabotaging these efforts. In these organizations, the indirect strategies will not work, or if they do, the positive outcomes will last for only a short period of time. These organizations sustain their position by arguing that the latest craze is only a craze that has no practical application in the business world. Their excuses for strategies not working are sometimes blamed on the strategies themselves. In other cases, there is an argument that the strategies would work if only 'they' lifted their game.

By way of example, I have come across situations where the UGRs sabotage indirect strategies such as the following:

- An organization initiated an employee of the month award that was scoffed at by staff. Unbeknown to management, the staff's view of management was so cynical that they regarded the award as a token effort that had no substance or genuine value. This strategy (the award) came from a manager who saw it being used in another organization, but the underlying UGR would not allow it to work. The award is displayed on the wall near the entrance with a degree of honour felt by management, who are blissfully unaware that staff do not regard it in nearly the same light

- An organization that commissioned a report to acquire staff attitudes about the most important aspects of the business – including levels of communication, involvement in decision making, rewards and recognition, and so on. When the report was completed, it showed extremely low levels of morale, so the report was shelved and literally kept under lock and key. At a superficial level, the management team was saying 'We're open and honest, and keen to get your views'. Of course, the UGR that was in operation was 'As a management team, we are only interested in staff feedback when it is positive'. Interestingly 'pirated' copies of this report were circulated among staff, and morale dropped even more

- An organization that commissioned a number of development programmes focussed on service, during which the management was openly negative and cynical. In essence the management looked for reasons why this could not work in their unique industry context. The UGR here is 'We're so different that nothing works'. This is a classic case of a management team not being prepared to undertake self analysis to determine why each of these programmes resulted in little change

In these and similar cases, the UGRs triumph. Putting even the best strategies in place will count for little if the UGRs are negative. Put simply, in most cases cultural change by osmosis does not work.

Direct Cultural Change Methods[*]

In many organizations, a *direct* approach is needed to address the issue of the organizational culture. The direct approach involves tackling the issue of culture explicitly – making culture a strategic priority for the team or entire organization. This is as much about process (i.e. who is involved and how) as it is content (i.e. what do we focus upon). For it to be successful, there must be involvement from as many staff as possible. It means creating staff and management understanding of corporate culture, getting

---

[*] I am very much indebted to Professor Ron Cacioppe, Managing Director of the Senior Management Centre in Western Australia, for the development of these change methods. His collaboration on various UGR-related projects has been invaluable and instructive.

their views, and involving them in creating a new and positive culture.

There is not an abundance of literature about organizations that have adopted the direct approach to cultural change, but a recent article[29] cites some substantial improvement in company performance based on what I would call the direct approach.

Vice Chairman and Director of Alberto-Culver, Carol Bernick attributes a company turn-around in sales and pre-tax profit to their focus on the company culture. In a process that was very inclusive, the company spelled out 'individual economic values' (IEVs) – short statements that describe how individuals contribute to profitability. One person's IEV for example is 'I turn every customer I talk to into a company fan'. In addition, ten 'cultural imperatives' were developed by staff, being honesty, ownership, trust, customer orientation, commitment, fun, innovation, risk taking, speed and urgency and teamwork. It is worth noting that in UGR parlance, these 'cultural imperatives' are abbreviated UGRs!

Bernick says:

> 'If there is one move I credit more than anything else for the success of the cultural makeover, it's our decision to create a role called Growth Development Leader (GDL). Each GDL (we now have about 70 at Alberto Culver North America) mentors a dozen or so people who may or may not be direct reports... I meet with the GDLs every six weeks or so. They are expected to bring forward their people's questions and concerns and, afterwards, to share with their groups the topics and solutions we've discussed. At most of the meetings, each group brings a group member as a guest. We talk about sales and earnings, new programs, workplace rumours, new product analyst ratings of our stock – whatever is on their minds and mine. We market the things we're doing well, and we aren't afraid to identify the things we're still doing poorly.'[30]

The turn-around in this company has, as its foundation, the cultural imperatives (or UGRs in our language), which were tackled directly.

In the following pages, I outline some of the *direct* cultural change strategies that have been used with different groups and organizations over the past few years, using UGRs as the vehicle. In a sense, there is logic to the sequencing, although implementation of all the strategies in a prescribed order is not necessary. Nonetheless, there are three broad phases through which organizations must proceed, these being 'Awareness', 'Action' and 'Ongoing focus and follow up'.

The First Phase: Awareness

Strategy 1A: Senior management introduction to the concept of UGRs

A cultural change programme using UGRs must begin with senior management and there must be a commitment to changing to more positive UGRs. It is widely understood that cultural change cannot occur without the direct and sustained involvement of senior management – and changing UGRs is no exception. Senior management need time to understand, synthesize and analyse the UGR concept, and to understand their unique role in creating and sustaining them.

Strategy 1B: Staff introduction to the concept of UGRs

Because organizational culture has been so widely misunderstood, I believe that exposure to the UGR concept is a major step towards achieving an improved culture. This is essential - being aware of the UGR concept creates a window of opportunity for staff, many of whom previously had given up hope of things ever changing. Remember, up to now the vast majority of staff and management have felt that they are subject to the powers of the corporate culture, without knowing what they could do about it. Having tried to challenge the culture, they have been 'pulled down the ladder' by the masses. Awareness of UGRs creates a simple alternative. Awareness gives hope, and hope can lead to action.

Strategy 2: Invite a person from another organization who has gone through a cultural change process to share their experience

In the early preparation for a cultural change programme, it can be useful to invite people from similar and other industries to share their insights into cultural change. Their sharing of successes, failures and ongoing difficulties can sharpen the mind of your people – and with your people's knowledge of UGRs, odds are they will understand with more clarity some of the problems and difficulties experienced by other organizations.

The Second Phase: Action

Strategy 3: Stocktake of existing UGRs

One strategy that can be undertaken, although with a degree of sensitivity and caution, is to get a 'fix' on prevailing UGRs. I have undertaken this with a number of groups, and have learned that anonymity must be preserved to get a true picture of existing UGRs.

One simple yet powerful strategy involves a simple 'complete the sentence' exercise. So far, I have used a number of these, including the following:

- Around here, customers are...
- Around here, customer complaints are...
- Around here, being open and honest gets you...
- Around here, when you criticise your boss...
- Around here, when it comes to spending money...

One idea is to ask staff and management to write their responses to these sentence lead-ins on index cards. They can then be collected and bundled together to ensure anonymity.

Table 3 below is a complete list of responses we received with regard to the sentence beginning 'Around here, customers are...'. The group comprised around 20 middle and senior managers across different local government authorities in Western Australia. The responses have been categorised in terms of being positively or negatively orientated, and whether or not they referred to the impact on, or treatment by the organization, or what the 'customers bring to us'.

The responses are extremely powerful in that they are so negatively focused. They show a tendency for customers to be viewed as intrusions on people's day-to-day work, with a much smaller proportion seeing customers as valuable or valued.

In each of these local government organizations, it would be reasonable to presume that there exists a large amount of documentation heralding the importance of customers. Indeed, in many of these organizations, standards of customer service would exist, and the provision of high levels of customer service would be included as an important part of job descriptions. Importantly, this documentation would count for nothing, if most staff shared the negative UGRs articulated by these middle and senior managers.

Table 3:
Categorised responses to the lead in sentence
'Around here, customers are…',
provided by middle and senior managers from various
Western Australian local government authorities

	Positive	Negative
Impact on, or treated by the organization	Valued and we respond as quickly as possible Valued Welcomed Increasing in importance So important that if you don't follow the Customer Service Charter you get the 'Big Stick' at you Important Listened to Respected and appreciated Always right	Unappreciated and have a lesser priority than day to day paperwork A disruption to real work A pain in the backside An interruption to getting my job done A necessary evil An intrusion on our work time Tolerated but not welcomed Important but interrupt work flow all too frequently Usually an interference to our work Often interruptions An "interruption" A pain in the neck
What they bring to us		Becoming increasingly demanding as a result of changing technology ie instant access = instant answers Uninformed with the processes involved in my division Uneducated ratepayers Valued, but they are not aware of the constraints we work under, so their opinion is uninformed

Table 4 below shows the categorised responses to the sentence beginning 'Around here, customer complaints are...', acquired from eight staff from an Australian bank. These responses show some positive UGRs – seeing complaints as a challenge and showing the need to listen to the customer's complaint, are encouraging. Nonetheless, there is also some cause for concern with regard to the perceived lack of support given to staff, and the need for staff not to 'hand on' the complaining customer so quickly. Again, documentation in the form of service standards and job descriptions is prominent in this bank. At least in some quarters, negative UGRs are undermining the intentions behind this documentation.

Table 4:

Categorised responses to the lead in sentence 'Around here, customer complaints are…', provided by staff from an Australian bank

	Positive	Negative
Source of the complaint		Usually day to day frustrations taken out on the staff... Normally about the long queuing time and lack of staff
Attitude of staff or organization to complaint	Usually not that bad and easily resolved by listening and understanding the customer, but sometimes the customers are really upset and rude and this is when the manager takes over Treated as a challenge. We cannot fix problems or customer difficulties if we do not know what they are or that they are happening. If we get a complaint and fix it, we will change the procedure so that it will not happen again Welcome, and should be looked on as a challenge	Very time consuming and sometimes very upsetting where you get no support to help you deal with them Acted on fairly promptly, however staff need to take more responsibility and not try to handball
Effect on staff		A pain in the neck, and can make you feel really drained. Some customers can make a big drama over a simple little thing

The final sample responses to lead in sentences are included in Table 5 below. These are responses to 'Around here, being open and honest gets you…'. The respondents were eight staff from an Australian State Government agency. Again they are very instructive in revealing the true UGRs driving some people within the organization.

Table 5:

Responses to the lead in sentence 'Around here, being open and honest gets you...', provided by staff from an Australian State Government agency

	Positive	Negative
All responses	Heard	Into difficulties. It often pays to be a bit guarded about comments, especially in cross-divisional meetings/situations
	A lot further. It builds confidence and trust in your other colleagues	
	Respect within certain circles. The honesty word is something I hear from disagreeable, complaining, whingeing co-workers as they character assassinate a fellow officer, the managers etc. Open and honest with reserves is the way to go	Nowhere. Although open communication is encouraged in our values and opinion poll results, in practice there is a long way to go, particularly by management
		In trouble
	There are some people I would love to be open and honest with. In my dealings with senior officers in the appropriate situation e.g. private conversations in offices, I have found it to be an invaluable communication style	Into situations where you need to be able to justify why things have occurred, thus helps to ensure processes and events have been conducted within policy

Strategy 4: Creating positive UGRs

In the process of familiarising people with the concept of UGRs, it is fruitful to get them to participate in the creation of their own positive UGRs. You can ask people in small groups to generate some positive UGRs and write them as though they already exist. The lead in to these should always be 'Around here.....', and people complete the sentence. After having done this with literally hundreds of people across a range of organizations, **I have never heard a positively framed UGR that other people have disagreed with!** Generating positive UGRs is an extremely uplifting experience for all involved.

The UGR list that is generated within any work team will reflect how people feel in the organization in terms of the culture they would like to have. As a guide, I have listed below the final outcomes from a programme that involved some 400 staff in one organization with which I worked. They generated UGRs that fell under four broad categories as follows:

As individuals, we are committed to internal and external service

- People say what they think and do what they say
- We are not afraid to give our opinions and discuss internal problems
- We are flexible
- Our attitude to problems is positive

We work in teams that are caring, functional and effective

- People are valued, made to feel valued and are rewarded for their efforts
- We support each other
- We are all treated as equals

- We accept each others' opinions
- We work in a team environment
- Enthusiasm, effort and initiative is acknowledged
- We respect individuality
- We recognise achievement of others
- Roles and responsibilities of staff are clearly defined and understood by the team
- We respect each other

Management is committed to customer service, effective communication and support for all staff

- There is honest open communication, without fear of retribution at all levels, and across all levels
- Management is without bias
- Decisions are carried through
- Staff concerns are listened to
- Management actions reflect management policies
- We support management and management supports us
- There is open communication with management
- We know what is going on

Our customers are our priority

- We care for the customer
- We value our clients
- We attend to customers quickly
- We seek customer involvement in our planning
- We care

The above list of preferred UGRs is lengthy, as you would expect from the collation of contributions from around 400 people. My personal preference would be to limit the number of preferred UGRs.

Strategy 5: 'Walk the Talk'

This would involve people's personal commitment to behaving in a way consistent with preferred UGRs. This is probably seen as a 'soft' strategy, yet if people genuinely commit to this, the impact would be substantial. Of course, securing a genuine commitment can be a difficult task.

Strategy 6: Senior management team commits to establish their own UGRs

The senior management team could consider the behaviours they need to display to be consistent with the preferred UGRs. They could keep them as private goals for each of the senior managers, or they could make them known across the organization.

Strategy 7: Generate a list of UGRs that work against the values statements incorporated as part of the Strategic Plan.

As was discussed earlier in this book, one useful strategy is to identify the UGRs that would work against achievement of each of the Values that typically form part of the strategic planning process. This process is a very good bridge to translate values - typically perceived as motherhood statements, into day to day behaviours.

The Third Phase: Ongoing focus and follow up

Strategy 8: UGRs as a standing agenda item for meetings

After getting people involved in the creation of their own UGRs, there is a real risk that the momentum will swing back to the old ways. Negatively framed UGRs have sometimes been the dominant force, and they will not change overnight. That is why some considerable effort needs to be invested into sustaining the push for positive UGRs.

One way to do this is to include UGRs as part of every second (or third, or whatever is deemed most appropriate) meeting for all teams. Five minutes can be dedicated towards discussion on how we are going with regard to the UGRs – and both positive and negative comment can be encouraged.

Putting them routinely on the agenda of meetings will again send a message that we are serious about UGRs.

Strategy 9: Team analysis of existing UGRs, linked to positive UGRs

This would involve your people making an assessment of how well the team is carrying out the highest priority preferred UGRs. The rating scale could be as simple as 'High', 'Medium' and 'Low', and each person in the team could be involved. The UGRs with a low rating would then be considered in terms of the specific action that could be implemented to improve performance.

I have done this with one team where there were some extremely severe performance and communication issues,

Can UGRs Be Changed?

and the team was effectively dysfunctional. In this case, we first generated UGRs that the team would like to have in place. They came up with the following list:

- We are *one* team
- We respect and value each other
- We are friendly, approachable and willing to help each other, even when the pressure is on
- We are well informed, and communication is open across all levels
- We value our customers and want to give them value
- We take pride in our work and get it right first time
- We work with our customers to *help* them, which means more than simply giving them information
- People are approached directly and constructively when there is a problem

We placed each UGR separately on flip charts around the room. I then asked each individual to rate two aspects of each UGR, ranging from 'High', through 'Medium' through 'Low':

- The importance of the UGR
- The current performance of the team

Before doing this, we discussed whether or not people wished to remain anonymous, or whether they would be prepared to place their initials as part of the rating system, so we could identify who felt how! They agreed to use their initials, and part of the outcomes are provided on the following page (Figure 3).

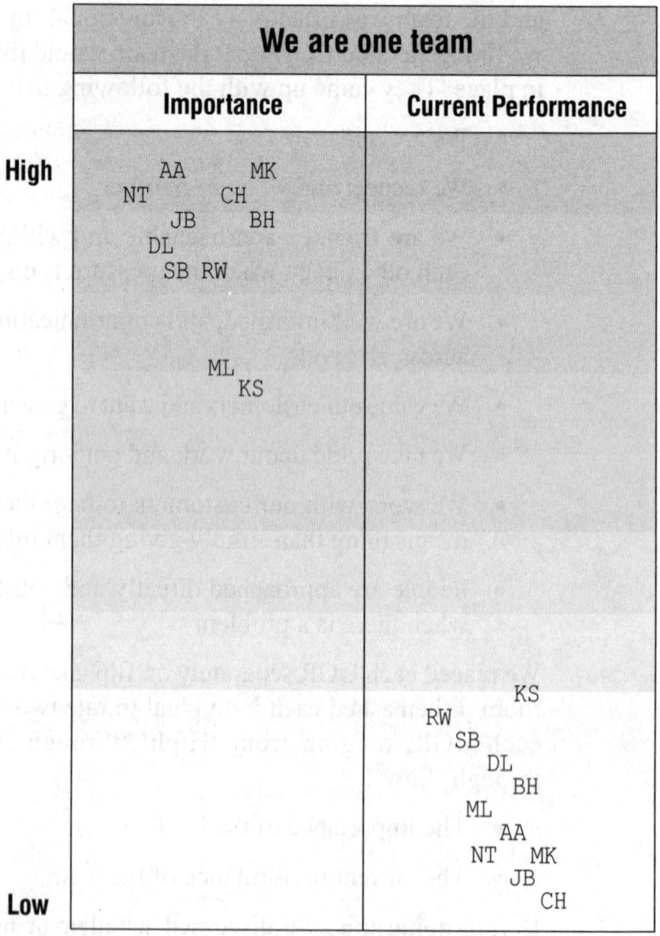

We are one team	
Importance	Current Performance
High 　　AA　　MK NT　　CH 　JB　BH DL SB RW 　　ML 　　　KS **Low**	 　　　　KS 　　RW 　　SB 　　　DL 　　　　BH 　　ML 　　　　AA 　　NT　MK 　　　JB 　　　　CH

Figure 3:
Staff ratings of importance and
current performance of selected UGRs

The above examples show that for the first UGR ('We are one team'), most staff rated this as being of 'High' importance, while most rated the team's current performance as 'Low'.

Following the ratings of each UGR, the team sat down and worked out where there were largest differences between 'importance' and 'current performance'. On the three UGRs where there were greatest differences, the team then decided on specific strategies that could be deployed to raise the team's performance.

This was a tough task, and it must be said that some tears were shed. One staff member decided she could no longer continue with the team and left the organization. It was however, the beginning of a dramatic improvement in the way in which the team functioned.

Twelve months after this exercise, exit interviews of 346 customers accessing the services provided by this team showed extremely high levels of customer satisfaction. Staff were rated by customers to have high levels of courtesy, friendliness and knowledge. The team was back on track.

Strategy 10: UGRs Incorporated as a standard procedure as part of each project implementation plan

If your team is involved in the implementation of new projects, there is an option to include consideration of UGRs as a 'standard procedure' for an implementation plan. All parties involved in generating the plan could give consideration to the most important UGRs that would be necessary for successful implementation of the plan.

Strategy 11: Ongoing feedback on performance against preferred UGRs

All staff could be surveyed annually (or whatever was deemed a suitable timeframe) to determine their perceptions of the team's and/or organization's performance against preferred UGRs. The instrument designed to undertake such a survey I conducted with one organization is included as Appendix 1.

Where to Start?

To assist in identifying the right mix of strategies for your organization or team, it is important to identify another key issue related to UGRs. This issue is to do with 'organizational alignment'.

There are two important variables when it comes to UGRs that have a major impact on how any organization performs – one variable is the current UGRs that exist in the team or organization, and the other important variable is the extent of 'positive talk' displayed by senior management.

I define 'positive talk' by senior management as the extent to which they engage in public (and to a degree one on one) conversations where the essence of the discussion is about positive aspects of the organization, or people within the organization. Those senior people who engage in positive talk are commonly regarded as positively oriented people, and even in situations that are difficult or challenging, they maintain a positive bias. This 'positive talk' is not fabricated – it is a manager's genuine view about a situation, group, or individual within the corporation.

From a logical standpoint, it is possible for an organization to have positive UGRs, with relatively low levels of 'positive talk' from senior management. Similarly, it is possible to have high levels of 'positive talk' from senior management while having negatively oriented UGRs. Indeed, from a staff perspective, we can consider these two dimensions and create an interesting matrix, displayed below.

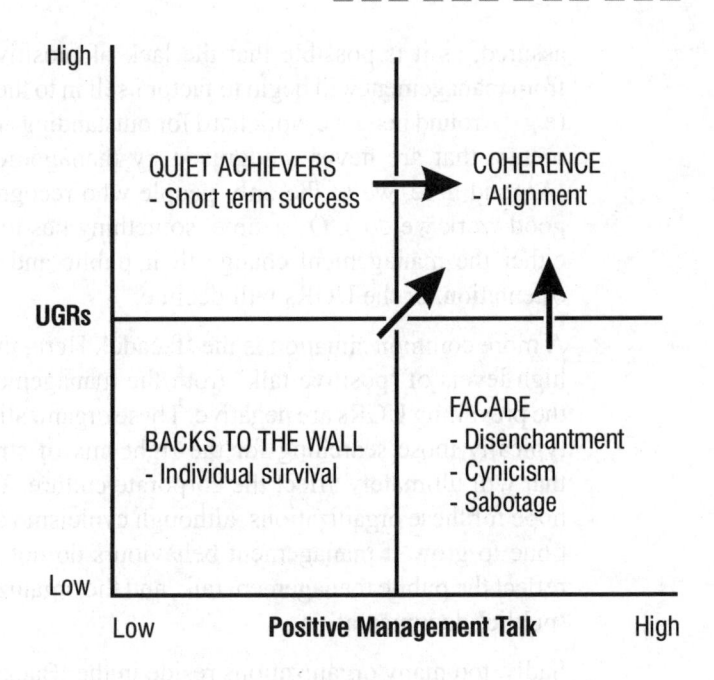

```
High │
     │   QUIET ACHIEVERS      COHERENCE
     │   - Short term success  - Alignment
     │                    ↗
UGRs │─────────────────────────────────
     │                    ↑
     │   BACKS TO THE WALL   FACADE
     │   - Individual survival  - Disenchantment
     │                          - Cynicism
     │                          - Sabotage
Low  │
     └─────────────────────────────────
       Low   Positive Management Talk   High
```

Figure 4:
UGR alignment matrix

In the above matrix, which represents the *staff* perspective on each variable, there are four broad sets of positions against which an organization can plot itself.

The 'Coherence' cell indicates that there are high levels of 'positive talk' by management, and UGRs are positively orientated. These organizations will grow and prosper because the external and internal messages are aligned, and positive.

The 'Quiet Achievers' cell represents those organizations or teams where management do not have an external positive orientation as seen by staff, but where UGRs are generally positive. The future of these organizations is not assured, as it is possible that the lack of 'positive talk' from management will begin to factor itself in to the UGRs (e.g. 'Around here, we work hard for outstanding achievements, that are never recognised by management', or 'Around here, we're the only people who recognise the good work we do'). Over time, something has to give – either the management change their public and private orientation, or the UGRs will decline.

A more common situation is the 'façade'. Here, there are high levels of 'positive talk' from the management, but the prevailing UGRs are negative. These organizations are typically those searching for the right mix of strategies that will ultimately affect the corporate culture. There is hope for these organizations, although cynicism will continue to grow if management behaviours do not start to reflect the public management talk, and the organization's 'public' documentation.

Sadly, too many organizations reside in the 'Backs to the Wall' cell. In these corporations, neither the UGRs nor the management orientation is positive. For whatever reasons, everyone has given up hope, and this is verbalised by management. The agenda in these organizations is self-preservation and self-advancement.

As the arrows show in Figure 3, the goal in any work context is to achieve alignment. Organizations that are located in the 'Coherence' cell are typically described as 'what you see is what you get', and there is a desire to be associated with, or belong to, these groups.

Once a team or organization is able to plot itself in this matrix, the types of strategies that need to be deployed to move to the 'Coherence' cell become evident. This is summarised below – again with the proviso that the recommended strategies should be read only as a guide.

Can UGRs Be Changed?

To Move From	To Coherence	Recommended Strategies (#'s)
Façade	Need to focus on changing the behaviour of management. In these contexts, management 'mouth the right words' but their actions do not reflect their talk. They need either to change their behaviour, or to change their talk, the former being preferable! A cultural change programme in this organization would focus firstly on management.	1A, 2, 5, 6, 7, 9, 11
Quiet Achievers	Need for management to begin to become more visibly involved talking about successes, being positive about achievements, being interested in individual and group accomplishments. Here again, a cultural change programme would need to start first with management.	1A, 2, 5, 6, 7, 9, 11
Backs to the Wall	There is a possibility that the people in management are not the right people for the job. If management are to remain however, they need to begin to establish a positive presence, and to begin talking about small successes (as they will only be small to begin with!). This re-orientation to the positive will need to be sustained and will need to be backed up by behaviour. Changes in the UGRs will not occur overnight. A cultural change programme in this type of corporation would need to begin with management, but would then need to incorporate all staff.	1A, 1B, 3, 4, 5, 8, 10, 11

In a Nutshell

- There are two ways in which Corporate Culture can be improved:
    - Indirect cultural change methods – where service-related or other improvement initiatives are introduced in the hope this will filter through to the culture

- Direct cultural change methods – where the issue of corporate culture is addressed explicitly. This is the approach that will yield best results
- A number of specific strategies that link to three logical phases of a cultural change strategy are summarised below:

Phase	No.	Strategy
The First Phase: Awareness	1A	Senior management introduction to the concept of UGRs
	1B	Staff introduction to the concept of UGRs
	2	Invite a person from another organization who has gone through a cultural change process to share their experience
The Second Phase: Action	3	Stocktake of existing UGRs
	4	Creating positive UGRs
	5	'Walk the talk'
	6	Senior management team commits to establish their own UGRs
	7	Generate a list of UGRs that work against the Values Statements incorporated as part of the strategic plan
The Third Phase: Ongoing focus and follow up	8	UGRs as a standing agenda item for meetings
	9	Team analysis of existing UGRs, linked to positive UGRs
	10	UGRs incorporated as a standard procedure as part of each project implementation plan
	11	Ongoing feedback on performance against preferred UGRs

- Organizations need not deploy each of these strategies, and they are not necessarily sequential. They should be chosen on the basis of what is most appropriate given the size, context and past history of the corporation

UGRs Into the Future

Three huge forces are now impacting on companies worldwide. Each of these forces has important implications for UGRs in the future. These forces are:

- The outcomes from an era of downsizing, mergers and acquisitions
- The 'new consumer'
- The Internet and e-commerce

Each of these forces, and the implications on UGRs, is discussed below.

Force #1 – The outcomes from an era of downsizing, mergers and acquisitions

The 1990's, like no other period to date, can be remembered as the 'downsizing' era. In the three year period, 1991 to 1994, massive job cuts were experienced across the US and elsewhere. Deal and Kennedy[31] provide a summary of job cutbacks in the US, which is replicated in Table 6 below.

Table 6:
25 largest downsizing, 1991-1994

Company	Staff Cutbacks
IBM	85,000
AT&T	83,500
GM	74,000
US Postal Services	55,000
Sears	50,000
Boeing	30,000
Nynex	22,000
Hughes Aircraft	21,000
GTE	17,000
Martin-Marietta	15,000
DuPont	14,800
Eastman Kodak	14,000
Philip Morris	14,000
Procter and Gamble	13,000
Phar Mor	13,000
Bank of America	12,000

Making the point that job losses did not stop at the end of this period, these same authors go on to report on an annual survey of the American Management Association (AMA):

> 'Moreover, in a separate survey conducted by the AMA in 1995, over 95% of the members indicated they were reengineering – presumably with more job cuts to come. As an indication that these intentions were real, in August 1998, Challenger, Gray and Christmas reported that 321,217 jobs had been eliminated in the United States in the first half of 1998 – a figure almost equal to the record-setting pace established in 1993. Cost cutting has truly come of age. For better or for worse, corporate cultures of the future will have to take this into account.'[32]

The advent of the shareholder value craze not only sparked cost cutting and downsizing. In 1981, the value of merger deals in the US surpassed $100 billion for the first time. By 1995 this figure had risen to more than $1 trillion. Two years later, this figure had almost doubled to $2 trillion. This exponential increase in the value of merger deals was similarly reflected in the number of merger deals.

So what has all this got to do with corporate culture? Plenty! In a context where individuals' futures are at risk and their positions are in doubt, organizational cultures can be shattered. Such fundamental change to the identity and structure of organizations has created levels of uncertainty and distrust which fuel new UGRs – the vast majority of which are negatively oriented. While not framed in UGR terms, the following says a great deal about the impact of downsizing, mergers and acquisitions on corporate culture:[33]

> 'Business specific knowledge is always lost in any large scale downsizing – and most managers must realise this. More serious is the reality that the corporate soul is often

wrenched out. With it goes the historical sense of how the company can succeed and prosper. In its place is a cultural vacuum – one filled by distrust and resentment.'

This force, which has impacted on both private and public sector organizations has had a profound impact on the mindset of many workers and managers. It has placed many organizations on the back foot when it comes to establishing a positive, service oriented culture. Importantly, it must be recognised as a major issue that needs to be dealt with as part of any improvement initiatives.

Force #2 – The 'New Consumer'

In their recent book, 'The Soul of the New Consumer'[34], Lewis and Bridger argue the demise of the 'Old Consumer' and the birth of the 'New Consumer'. Old Consumers, it is argued, were beset with scarcities of cash, choice and availability. The New Consumer is now faced with scarcities of time, attention and trust.

This shift in 'scarcities' has caused a change in business – consumer interactions that are fundamental and far reaching. Unless corporations understand these changes, their futures are going to be seriously challenged.

New Consumers are people with disposable income who are now much more discerning, and who desire authenticity over convenience.

Businesses in the past could rely on convenience marketing – mass marketing and mass consumption characterised the business relationship with the consumer. These Old Consumers had limited choice, and often purchased products and services out of habit.

But things have changed.

The New Consumers, with financial muscle, have signalled a dramatic change in their purchasing processes. More educated, and increasingly averse to traditional marketing methods, New Consumers are more individual, involved, independent and informed.

A shift towards 'authenticity' can be seen in many instances – the rise of Starbucks as an authentic coffee house and the success of boutique breweries, are two examples.

> 'Over the next decade companies producing only commodities may find themselves struggling to survive in a marketplace increasingly dominated by intense global competition and falling prices, while those able to satisfy the New Consumers' appetite for authenticity will flourish.'[35]

Marketing to the Old Consumer was relatively simple. It was called 'mass marketing'. The power of this approach is being seriously diminished however by the New Consumer.

> 'No more holding people hostage through 30-second commercials. No more hype. No more ignorant customers. No more local monopolies. No more search costs. No more 'Get in your car and come to us'. If you're paying attention, you're sweating by now.'[36]

New Consumers are also characterised by their need for involvement. This even translates into their choices in grocery shopping, where they actively involve themselves in safeguarding their family's health, and where they show their environmental and ethical positions. They exercise these choices in part because they are well informed. Access to the Internet, as well as a variety of other sources, has resulted in reading more of the details of labels than ever before.

Lewis and Bridger summarise differences between Old and New Consumers in the following way[37]:

Old Consumer	New Consumer
Seek convenience	Seek authenticity
Synchronised	Individual
Less often involved	Involved
Conformist	Independent
Less well informed	Well informed

The UGR implications of the New Consumer phenomenon are far reaching, and go beyond the Marketing Department in companies. The 'conventional wisdom' about customers may no longer be 'wisdom'. Corporations will need to have a culture in place that challenges the assumptions made about customer segmentation, and customer preferences. The culture will need to be characterised by constant questioning, by being in touch with developments within and without the industry, and by an appetite for customer feedback – both positive and negative.

Force #3 – The Internet and e-commerce

The Internet is the biggest single thing to affect our economic and social institutions. It is a revolutionary technology that now affects computer users and non-users alike.

The power of the Internet is much greater than the simple questions of 'if and how' businesses should engage in e-commerce. Indeed, Kanter[38] argues that the Internet is re-shaping society in a number of ways:

- Network power – where, potentially, everyone is connected to everyone else. 'Network reach' is now more important than size

- Transparency and direct communication – there is now greater visibility and fast, rapid information access

- Fast feedback, easy protest – customers are able to provide immediate feedback, and groups can galvanise very quickly to voice their concerns

- Constant change and reliance on new knowledge – there is now extreme competition for the newest skills and the newest talent – perhaps for the first time, skilled young people are in high demand as a major source for groups to be at the 'leading edge'

- Large audiences and crowd behaviours – geography is increasingly an irrelevant barrier as messages can reach vastly larger audiences. Messages can spread much further

These fundamental changes create the *imperative* for organizations to respond appropriately – they are so wide reaching that there is no longer an *option* not to change.

It is not surprising however, that in many companies there are strong internal barriers to change. Interestingly, these internal barriers are more prominent in organizations that have been in existence for longer periods. Kanter[39] undertook research into the barriers to e-culture and e-business change. Some of the key results are provided in Table 7 below:

Table 7:

Selected barriers to change in older and newer organizations

Barrier	Org's Older than 20 Years (n=390)	Org's Younger than 20 Years (n=395)
	Percentage of respondents	
The unit does not have staff with adequate technical or web-specific skills	48	27
Customers and key markets do not want to change their behaviour	37	37
Employees are not comfortable with change	29	20
Leaders are not sure where to begin; they don't understand how to make the right choices	30	12
Top executives do not personally use computers and are not personally familiar with the Internet	22	10
Rivalries or conflicts between internal divisions	22	9
Managers fear loss of status or privileged positions	17	7

These results in one sense should hardly be surprising. The culture in older organizations is more likely to be entrenched, and whilst a resilient culture can be a strength, it can also be the reason behind a company's demise.

These change resistors are very worrying given Kanter's[40] view:

> 'E-culture defines the human side of the global information era, the heart and soul of the New Economy. People and organizations everywhere must evolve to embrace this business culture of tomorrow – no matter where they are on the continuum of Internet use.
>
> Taking full advantage of the potential of the Internet Age requires leaders to lead differently and people to work together in new configurations.'

This same author goes on to argue that a culture for change needs to be programmed into the organization's operations:

> 'Leaders must thus reset the organization's default position. They must change the template and get to the underlying code. To become an e-business, David Weymouth, CIO of Barclays bank in the UK said 'You've got to be prepared to change the genetic code of the organization.'[41]

Of course, this has wide ranging implications for the UGRs in organizations of the future. Kanter cites her research that involved 785 companies in a global e-culture survey. Those companies indicating that they were better than competitors displayed cultural characteristics that shed light on the UGRs that will be necessary for success in the future:

- Internal changes are considered a way of life, and people seem to take them in their stride (instead of viewing them as disruptive, inconvenient, or a source of discomfort)
- Conflict is seen as creative and something to be encouraged (instead of disruptive and something to be avoided)

- Ideas that are unusual, controversial, or 'different' are strongly encouraged and well received (instead of being viewed with scepticism and resistance)

- When the organization is considering a more strategic change, most people generally hear about it in advance, so they have the chance to comment (instead of learning about change at the same time as outsiders, or even later)[42]

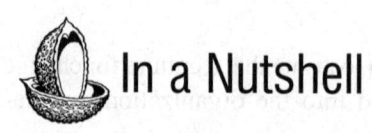

In a Nutshell

Three major forces impact on current UGRs in organizations, the directions and the way in which corporate cultures need to move in the future:

- The outcomes from an era of downsizing, mergers and acquisitions – the organizational re-engineering of the 1990s has left in its wake a culture of uncertainty and distrust. In creating a more positive, service focussed culture, corporations will need to recognise that the mindset of many workers and managers is negatively orientated – often for good reasons!

- The 'New Consumer' – consumers of today are substantially different from consumers of 20 years ago. The 'New Consumer' faces scarcities of time, attention and trust yet at the same time they have financial muscle. These characteristics must be responded to in different ways, and it is imperative that organizations change accordingly. The old ways of marketing and responding to customer needs will no longer succeed. UGRs about customers must be challenged if companies are to prosper

- The advent of the Internet has fundamentally changed social and economic institutions and communication networks across the globe. These changes mean that companies must respond, yet there is strong internal resistance to change in many organizations, particularly those corporations that have been in existence for 20 or more years. Paradoxically, in these older organizations, the cultural forces that have contributed to their success in the past may very well be the reasons for future failures. Successful organizations of the future will need to be characterised by UGRs that:

  - Recognise change as a constant, and as a 'way of life'
  - Value conflict
  - Encourage unusual and different ideas
  - Involve people in change with sufficient time before the event

UGRs – The Final View

Recently, I was working with a team, and going through the various issues associated with UGRs. Having considered the implications of UGRs, I organised people into smaller groups and asked them to talk about, and note down positive UGRs that they would like to see in place.

As usual, I asked people to complete the sentence 'Around here...'

After spending some time considering their preferred UGRs, I got each small group to share the ideas that they had come up with. As is often the case, each of the groups came up with an impressive list of preferred UGRs.

After the last group had shared the outcomes from their discussion, I challenged the group to consider what it would be like if the UGRs they had just created actually described their organization. I proposed that work would be a genuinely rewarding and enjoyable experience for all staff if those UGRs were in place.

At this stage, a participant named Alan asked a question that stopped me in my tracks. He asked, 'Steve, do you know of an organization where the UGRs are like those we have just created?'

I responded with another question – 'Why do you ask Alan?'

Alan's response was genuine, and not driven by cynicism. He said 'Because it's not possible is it?'

I often relate this story to groups with whom I work, and ask people how they would have responded to Alan's question. I get interesting suggestions that include:

- 'No, it's not possible'
- 'It isn't possible if you don't think it is'
- 'Yes, it is possible, as I have actually worked in a team with UGRs just like those we have just generated'

My response was slightly different from each of these. I said 'Alan, would your organization be better off if 80% of your people were doing 80% of the UGRs that we've just generated?'

Of course, his response was 'Yes'.

To which I responded 'Well it's simply a matter of **are these worth fighting for?**...'

To this day, I am not sure if a team exists anywhere where the UGRs are all positive. As individuals, we all have different needs and expectations, and in some cases these will be conflicting, even when we are working towards the same goals. Despite having been in more than 30 organizations to host 'Customer Service Study Tours', and despite having worked directly with over 100 different organizations over the last few years, I could not with any degree of confidence say to Alan that I had come across a work team where all the UGRs were positive.

I can be sure about one thing however. Those organizations and teams that leave things to chance will not succeed in the medium to long term. Those organizations that manufacture their future will more likely realise a successful one.

This principle is never more prominent than in the case of an organization's culture.

The development of the UGR concept has a long way to go. This book marks the beginning - the concept needs to be further explored, analysed, researched and fine tuned to enable more practical applications to emerge. At this stage I am in no position to proclaim miraculous success stories from corporations implementing the UGR concept!

Nonetheless, I have seen some substantial culture improvements following our work with UGRs – none more so than in what might seem initially a relatively trivial and isolated event. Let me explain...

I had been invited by the Human Resources Manager of a medium sized organization to run a series of one-day seminars with all staff. A major portion of the one-day seminar was to be devoted to introducing and working on UGRs. A total of nine training days were organised to run over a two week period.

On the second of the training sessions, the Human Resources Manager (let's call him Gary) approached me during the lunch break and asked whether he could speak to me privately. We went into his office and he informed me that he would not be remaining with the organization – he had found another position with another company, and wanted to inform me directly after building up a working relationship in preparation for the seminar programme. He asked me to keep the news confidential. Of course I agreed, and I congratulated him.

When I went in the next day, I was startled to see that Gary's office was completely vacated. Gary had packed up everything and gone. With what must have been a look of shock on my face, I approached Gary's most senior person (let's call her Janet) and said 'Janet, what's happened with Gary?'

With a degree of hesitation, Janet said 'Steve, there was an amicable agreement between the CEO and Gary'. I immediately knew this was not the real story, but I left it at that and went on to run the seminar.

Janet subsequently attended one of the remaining seminars and was helping pack my car after I had completed the ninth and final session. I thanked her for her help and support, and just as I was about to get into my car, said 'By the way Janet, what was the real story with Gary?'

This time without hesitation she said, 'There was an amicable agreement between the CEO and Gary'.

As I got into my car, I had a big smile on my face. I didn't look back at Janet, but I'm sure she had a smile on her face as well. This I regard as one of my best 'wins' with respect to UGRs. Janet was very clearly demonstrating she had taken the concept to heart, because she was living by a UGR that said:

Around here, we don't air our dirty linen in public

Janet knew what she was doing, and she knew that I knew – it was great!

This true story is the essence of UGRs. For too long, managers and staff have been fighting to achieve change in *other* people. The power of UGRs lies in the fact that we all as individuals choose to live by, or fight against UGRs. The UGR challenge is as much individual as it is strategic.

Armed with an understanding of UGRs, teams can now tackle the issue of culture with confidence. In the knowledge that a team's culture is not a complex, academic and theoretical concept, groups can now work on their culture in a positive and productive way.

In so doing, an organization has the chance to unlock potential that can truly create a service revolution.

Appendix 1

Sample Feedback Sheet on Collated UGRs

UGRs at the XXX Organization

During each of the 17 one-day customer service courses run for the XXX Organization, all of you were involved in recording sets of 'Unwritten Ground Rules' (UGRs) that you would like to see in place. These are statements that reflect how you 'would like to see things around here'.

The outcomes from the 17 courses have been analysed and summarised. These fall into three broad headings as follows:

We are committed as individuals
We work in effective and functional teams
Our customers are our priority

We would like to generate a permanent set of UGRs for the company, as a constant reminder of *'This is the way we do things around here'*.

Would you kindly review the attached list, which is a set of proposed UGRs, and indicate whether or not you think each UGR should be included?

There is also space for you to write additional UGRs that you would like included.

If you place your name at the top of this page (optional!), you will be in the prize draw for XXX.

Your completed feedback can be put into the marked box in the entrance to HR – we need these BY NO LATER THAN COB OCTOBER 13th.

Thanks in anticipation!

Your Name (Optional): _____

WE ARE COMMITTED AS INDIVIDUALS	Indicate YES or NO, whether you think these should be our permanent UGRs	
	YES (✓)	NO (✗)
We stay positive, even in the face of adversity		
We do what we say we will do		
We look for solutions not problems		
We do not let internal problems get in the way of meeting the customer's needs		
We support others as they work with their customers		
We accept feedback from customers as opportunities to improve		

WE WORK IN EFFECTIVE AND FUNCTIONAL TEAMS	Indicate YES or NO, whether you think these should be our permanent UGRs	
	YES (✓)	NO (✗)
We treat each other with respect		
We encourage each other		
Management lead by example		
Staff value management		
Teamwork is recognised and encouraged		
Communication is open and reaches all levels		
Skills are recognised, as are people's limitations		
Good performance is acknowledged		
We share responsibility		
We listen to others' views and ideas		
We encourage creativity		
We have fun		

OUR CUSTOMERS ARE OUR PRIORITY	Indicate YES or NO, whether you think these should be our permanent UGRs	
	YES (✓)	NO (✗)
We value our customers		
We treat our customers with respect and courtesy		
We treat our customers with sincerity		
We say thank-you		
We are focussed on meeting our customers' needs		

Notes

[1] Kotter, John P. and James L. Heskett, Corporate Culture and Performance, 1992, The Free Press, New York

[2] Deal, Terrence, and Allan Kennedy, The New Corporate Cultures, 2000, TEXERE Publishing Limited, London, p23

[3] Ibid., p25

[4] Schein, Edgar, Organizational Culture and Leadership, 1992, Jossey-Bass, p5

[5] Schein, Edgar, 1983, The role of the founder in creating organizational cultures, Organizational Dynamics, Summer: 13-29.

[6] Deshpande, R. and Webster, F. Jr., 1989, Organizational Culture and Marketing: Defining the Research Agenda, Journal of Marketing, 53, Jan., p5

[7] Borgatti, S., 1996, Corporate Culture Defined, at http://analytictech.com/mbo21/culture.htm

[8] Australian Customer Service Association, *How do you develop a service of culture within your organization?* Customer Magazine, June 1999, 24-27

[9] As a side note, I am intrigued by a general lack of understanding of 'vision' and 'mission' statements. I have read many 'vision' statements that specify the core business of the organization, whilst some 'mission' statements specify a vision, or detail strategies the organization intends to deploy. This is area in itself crying out for improvement!

[10] Lewis, Davis and Darren Bridger, The Soul of the New Consumer, Nicholas Brealey Publishing, 2000, p52-53

[11] I first came across a derivation of this term in a book by Karl Albrecht, *Service Within*, (Business One Irwin, USA, 1990) who cites a definition of culture as 'This is the way we do things around here'. Albrecht writes that the originators of this definition were Terrance Dean and Allan Kennedy in their book *Corporate Cultures*

[12] Pfeffer, Jeffrey and Robert I. Sutton, *The Smart-Talk Trap*, Harvard Business Review, May-June 1999

[13] Harvey, Jerry B., The Abilene Paradox and Other Meditations on Management, 1988, Jossey-Bass, San Francisco

[14] High, Gary, in The Knowing Doing Gap, Jeffrey Pfeffer and Robert I. Sutton, Harvard Business School Press, 2000, p83

[15] Pfeffer, Jeffrey and Robert I. Sutton, The Knowing Doing Gap, Harvard Business School Press, 2000, p85

[16] Semler, Ricardo, *Maverick : The Success Story Behind the World's Most Unusual Workplace,* Warner Books, Reprinted 1995

[17] I am fascinated by this tendency. I was 8 years old when I changed primary schools, and learned about this UGR – 'The way to turn people off is to relate stories that begin with the words, 'Well back in my old school...'. After learning this I avoided it as much as possible. Incredibly, many managers have yet to grasp this when they change organizations. They turn people off by saying 'Well, back in XXX organization, what we did was...'

[18] Peak Performance, Clive Gilson, Mike Pratt, Kevin Roberts and Ed Weyms, Harper Collins Business, London, 2000

[19] Daphne Pirie, a member of the board of directors, Ibid., p121

[20] Brian Glencross, High Performance Manager, Australian Institute of Sport, Ibid., p122

[21] Sharon Buchanan, past player under coach Charlesworth, Ibid., p123

[22] Coach Charlesworth, Ibid., pp124-125

[23] Keith Brown, Ibid., p144

[24] Tim Hallam, Senior Director of Media Services, Ibid., p146 and 148

[25] Keith Brown, Senior Director of Sales, Ibid., p154

[26] David Moffett, CEO, Ibid., p111

[27] Jack Ralston, Director of Commercial and Marketing, Ibid., p112

[28] Jack Ralston, Director of Commercial and Marketing, Ibid., p112-113

[29] Bernick, Carol Levin, When Your Culture Needs a Makeover, Harvard Business Review, June 2001, p5-11

[30] Ibid., p8

[31] Deal, Terrence, and Allan Kennedy, The New Corporate Cultures, 2000, TEXERE Publishing Limited, London, p70

[32] Ibid., p72

[33] Ibid., p85-86

[34] Lewis, Davis and Darren Bridger, The Soul of the New Consumer, Nicholas Brealey Publishing, 2000

[35] Ibid., p40

[36] Hamel, Gary and Jeff Sampler, The e-corporation, Fortune, December, 1998

[37] Lewis, Davis and Darren Bridger, The Soul of the New Consumer, Nicholas Brealey Publishing, 2000, p19

[38] Kanter, Rosebeth Moss, e-Volve, Harvard Business School Press, 2001, p16

[39] Ibid., p85

[40] Ibid., p7

[41] Ibid., p233

[42] Ibid., p230

About the Author

SOCAP in Europe have described Steve Simpson as 'the leading Australian Customer Care Guru'. UK based e-Customer Service World call Steve 'Australia's Corporate Culture guru'.

Perhaps these accolades explain why Steve is in demand across the globe as a keynote speaker and consultant.

He has featured at two World Conferences on Customer Service Management in the US where rated in the top 10 speakers. In addition, he has featured at the European Conference on Customer Management in London, the North American Conference on Customer Management in the US and other major conferences in the Australia, New Zealand, the UK, the US, India, South Africa, Malaysia and Singapore.

Steve has been accredited as a Certified Speaking Professional (CSP), the highest speaker distinction recognised by the International Federation for Professional Speakers.

He is author of the book 'Service Into Profit' and a contributing author to the 2004 book, The Power of Culture.

Steve's clients include Alcan, Lexus, Goldfields South Africa, the Royal Bank of Scotland, Bayer, Zurich, the Commonwealth Bank of Australia, Flight Centre, the Australian College of Health Service Executives, the Academy of Chief Executives in the UK, various educational organizations and a range of local, state and federal government agencies.

Steve heads up Keystone Management Services and can be contacted via details below:

Keystone Management Services
PO Box 554
Sanctuary Cove 4212
Queensland, Australia
Phone: +61 (0)7 5530 1465
Fax: +61 (0)7 5530 1295
Email: info@keystone-management.com
Web: www.keystone-management.com

Testimonials

There are speakers who speak well and then there are speakers that inspire and delight. Steve is the latter of the two. That room was "alive" when Steve finished. I just wanted to express my appreciation to Steve. There are so many talented people in this world, but not all of them have the ability to share it with others in such a magical way.

Stacey Robbins - **Health Alliance Medical Plans,** *Illinois, USA*

I've seen a lot of presenters at a lot of conferences - but few with the skills, the humour and the engaging cheek of Steve Simpson.

Phillip Adams, AO - Broadcaster, writer and film-maker

I attended a seminar recently at the Perth Concert Hall. One of the principal speakers was Steve Simpson whose presentation I considered to be one of the best that I have ever seen not only in Australia but around the world. I have no hesitation in saying that Steve Simpson is one of the best in the business. He is so impressive. I commend him highly.

Judge John Gotjamanos, Perth, Western Australia

I had the great pleasure of attending one of Steve's presentations at the European Customer Management Conference in London - I am so pleased that I chose his session. The UGRs concept has given me the **key** I have been searching for. Steve was inspirational.

Karen E Berry - **Halifax Bank of Scotland**

What an inspiration! I am already preparing a presentation for my Management Team to introduce them to some of your ideas with serious revolution in mind.

Cathy Carr - **Draeger Safety Pacific Pty Ltd,** *Melbourne, Victoria*

Frequently Asked Questions...

Here are some of the most common questions we are asked after people have been exposed to the concept of UGRs...

Q: Is there any more information on UGRs?

A: There is now a growing body of information about UGRs. A 15-minute video that features Steve Simpson introduces the concept of UGRs - this is available via the Keystone Management Services' web site (www.keystone-management.com). We also distribute the very popular monthly *Cultural Intelligence* newsletter, a large part of which is dedicated to UGRs. You can subscribe free of charge at the Keystone web site. Back copies of the newsletter are also available at this site.

There is also now a UGRs web site - www.UGRs.net, which contains a number of articles, an information video about UGRs, as well as the Cultural Intelligence newsletter.

Q: How can I obtain more copies of this book?

A: The book can be ordered on line at www.keystone-management.com. Send an email to info@keystone-management.com if you would like to discuss discounts for bulk orders.

Q: How can I book Steve as a speaker at my next conference or seminar?

A: Steve is a dynamic and sought after speaker, who presentations focus on leading edge customer service issues and of course, UGRs! Send an email to info@keystone-management.com or call any of the following numbers:

In Australia: +61 (0)7 5530 1465
In the UK: +44 (0)20 7870 6227
In the US: +1 (310) 601-8308

www.keystone-management.com